CLEARING THE AIR

How the people of Virginia improved the State's air and water despite the EPA

Becky Norton Dunlop

Published by the Alexis de Tocqueville Institution
and the Northumberland Echo

ISBN 0-9705485-0-8

Cover design: Peggy K. Chang
Front cover photograph: James K. Lacy
Back cover photograph: Chad Hunt

ii

To George S. Dunlop, my husband and best friend

Table of Contents

Foreword

As a citizen of the Commonwealth of Virginia employed by EPA for more than 20 years now, I feel privileged to have the opportunity to offer a few comments about this informative and insightful narrative of how a fellow conservative brought some common sense and considerable political acumen to the task of bringing Virginia cost-effectively into compliance with federal environmental regulations.

I was not acquainted with Becky Norton Dunlop during her tenure with the Reagan Administration. But after George Allen was elected Governor in 1993 and appointed Becky as Virginia's Secretary of Natural Resources, I and my fellow conservatives within EPA soon took notice of how effective she was in successfully challenging some of the arbitrary policies the Agency was trying to impose upon Virginia and other States. At least part of her success may be attributed to her confidence that she had the full support and backing of Governor Allen. This contrasts sharply with the support afforded Anne Gorsuch Burford, who as EPA Administrator had vowed to cut through bureaucratic red tape and enforce regulatory reform. After following marching orders from President Reagan's advisors to test Executive Privilege, she became politically expendable and was left twisting slowly in the wind.

As the owner-driver of an auto licensed in Virginia, I was especially pleased with her success in blocking EPA's attempt to force (blackmail) Virginia into centralized auto emission testing and the use of specific test equipment. Her determined defense of the continued use of decentralized state-supervised testing at local service stations reminded me of President Reagan's strategy for control of nuclear weapons during the cold war—"trust but verify."

I was also impressed with her success in decentralizing the Department of Environmental Quality (DEQ) by establishing field offices that could deliver local one-stop service to Virginia citizens and businesses trying to comply with environmental regulations, particularly with requirements for air, water and solid waste permits. While in Washington on one occasion, she accepted my invitation to speak to EPA employees about how Virginia's DEQ had been decentralized to serve its citizens "where the rubber meets the road." I fear her remarks fell largely on deaf ears, since the devolution of central authority could be expected to have no more appeal in Washington than it did among the DEQ bureaucrats formerly ensconced in Richmond.

I was interested to learn of all the legal maneuvering and political intrigue behind the Smithfield Foods case. From what I knew of the discharge from Smithfield Foods' wastewater treatment facility, it did not appear to be a huge threat to water quality in the Pagan River. What it all boiled down to ultimately was the question of whether Virginia, which has been delegated permitting authority by EPA, can be pre-empted by EPA in prosecuting violations of a permit issued by the State. Obviously, EPA's actions in this case were heavily tainted with power politics.

I perceived the Avtex Fibers facility in Front Royal as an "environmental catastrophe" only in the sense that it had become a huge regulatory liability for Virginia. The real issue in this case was not that it represented much of a threat to the environment, but who would pay for remediating the abandoned facility (removing materials that regulations had designated as "hazardous" waste) to bring it in tune with Superfund standards. Becky Norton Dunlop and her legal supersleuths deserve much credit for relieving Virginia of paying this bill.

Someone once observed that in the implementation of idealistic environmental legislation: Science tells us what can be done; economics tells us what should be done; but politics tells us what will be done. This book contains a number of excellent examples of how politics plays a major role in determining both the scope of environmental regulations developed at EPA and the Agency's enforcement policies.

—**Hugh Wise**
Scientist

"Clearing the Air"—a prologue

August 4, 1999
Washington, D.C.

Scanning my e-mail, I had a fleeting sense of *déjà vu*. There was a message from Jay Timmons, who had been chief of staff to Virginia Governor George Allen when I was Allen's Secretary of Natural Resources. I used to hear from Timmons almost every day, passing along the governor's responses to memoranda, asking questions, dispensing guidance and encouragement. But now, Allen had been out of office nearly 19 months. I was a vice president at the Heritage Foundation and a senior fellow with the Alexis de Tocqueville Institution. Timmons was working as a consultant in Richmond. Seeing his name atop the email, though, it felt as though I was about to receive news about the governor.

"Don't miss today's *R-T-D*," he wrote, using our abbreviation for the *Richmond Times-Dispatch*, the most influential newspaper in the state of Virginia. Timmons knew that I, up in Washington now, might. Back home in Arlington, I only occasionally read "the *R-T-D*."

As the Allen Administration's point man, Timmons knew our environmental record had been maligned. As recently as the month before, the Sierra Club had blamed "the sinister machinations of the Allen Administration" for a bureaucratic deficiency resulting from a previous governor's budget cuts. Worse: Certain media lent credence to mendacity by reporting such comments with glee.

All the more reason why today's story in the *Times-Dispatch* was as stunning as it was thrilling. A gush of oxygen filled my lungs as I looked at the front-page headline:

CLEARING THE AIR

The actual banner was even larger: it was set in 66-point type; the typeface above is 48 point. It was about the same size as the headlines that ran on the day America won the Gulf War, and larger than headlines over the nomination of Albert Gore and George Bush for president in the summer of 2000. Figuratively, readers were being told to sit down, to expect the unexpected—to prepare themselves for a story that would shatter conventional wisdom. If the lengthy subtitle was true to its promise, they would not be disappointed. It read:

"A Virginia Commonwealth University study has measured, for the first time, state environmental progress… using a statistically valid method.

"The study, which covered 1985-1998 for most issues, looked at trends statewide and showed Virginia's environmental health declined until 1994, then started improving."

1994—that was the year George Allen took office. No one, certainly not a member of Allen's team, would ever claim all the credit for such a turnaround belonged to the government. Still, considering our opposition had often claimed the Allen Administration would reverse years of progress, and wreck the environment, the story in the *R-T-D* was arresting.

Nor was the gist of these findings news to me. I knew we had made progress during the Allen years, and was confident that the facts of this success would be known eventually. Coming, however, from a truly scientific examination of the environment's real quality—a thing that is too rare in these debates—the findings gave me a real boost. And the prominence given them, in a story by one of the state's most respected papers, gave the scientific facts an added boost.

George Allen took office in 1994. The environment improved on his watch. For me there was a deep sense of satisfaction. We—the Allen Administration and the people of Virginia—had improved the environment. We did it in the face of sometimes bitter criticism and shrill warnings that our policies would do the opposite. And the fact that the environment had improved on our watch was being acknowledged.

1. Allen's revolution

When Ronald Reagan came to Washington in 1980, one of his themes was that he wanted to bring people into his administration who hadn't necessarily sought a position there. It wasn't just that the federal government had become tired and complacent, although it had. Ronald Reagan's philosophy was that government existed to serve the people—not the other way around—and that as such, it should bring in talented people from all walks of life. If you believe in this idea of service to people, you're not looking for someone who is out to build a political or bureaucratic empire. You want folks who come into government to do a job, to help the community, and return to private life.

My own entry into the Allen Administration in Virginia, I'm happy to say, happened to follow that model. I certainly wasn't looking for a job in Richmond. I had worked on the 1980 campaign of Ronald Reagan and served the full eight years of his administration, taking assignments in the White House and the Departments of Justice and Interior. The experience was exhilarating, one of the best in my life. It was also a lot of hard work, however, and a lot of government for someone of my philosophy.

When Allen was elected in the fall of 1993, I was working as managing director of an anti-pornography campaign, Enough Is Enough! I also wrote occasionally on environmental issues, having served as a founding director of the National Wilderness Institute and a senior fellow for environment and natural resources for the Citizens for a Sound Economy, a leading Washington think tank.

In short, I was quite content, and indeed busy, with various pursuits.

Even so, when a friend called and invited me to submit some personal information in order to serve as an advisor to the Allen transition, I must admit I wasn't reluctant. During his campaign, Allen struck me as someone who shared Ronald Reagan's populist vision, both as to what government should do and how people in government should do it. What's more he exuded confidence and optimism that it could be done. He was serious, in the best sense of the word.

So I packaged together a resume and sent it in. My husband, George, who had also been contacted, did the same. But neither one of us did a lot of tailoring or adapting, because we presumed we were talking about a position on some oversight commission or state board or the like—or a role literally advising Allen, but not as a member of his top staff.

To my mild surprise, Betsy Beamer, the Deputy Director of the Transition for the governor-elect called in late November and asked if I would be willing to come down to Richmond and discuss a position with his Administration. I said that I was flattered, but busy with enough other pursuits that really only a cabinet position would be of interest. I expected that Allen had basically filled his cabinet positions—that what I said would more or less lead to a polite end to the conversation. Instead, Mrs. Beamer, without missing a beat responded, "Okay—can you be here tomorrow?" This was the first but certainly not the last time I would be party to the calm, well-organized and efficient professionalism of Betsy Beamer who became Secretary of the Commonwealth. It was the inauspicious beginning of a friendship and professional relationship that is one of the incalculable rewards for me of working in the Allen Administration.

At our meeting, I could see that Allen was familiar with environmental issues. He was also well prepared. He knew about my experience in the Reagan Administration, during which I had been an Assistant Secretary of the Interior for Fish, Wildlife, and Parks with Interior Secretary Don Hodel. (I was also a presidential assistant in the White House, including work as an adviser on environmental issues to the President and his Cabinet and to Attorney General Ed Meese in his capacity as Counselor to the President for Domestic Policy and later as Attorney General.) Allen asked specific questions about my experience, particularly at Interior, that showed he had done his homework on me—and that he had some general ideas about what he wanted to accomplish as governor in the realm of environmental policy.

As we discussed opportunities for improving Virginia's environment, Allen and I realized we shared, among other things, admiration for President Reagan, a dread of oppressive government, and commitment to principles that had worked so marvelously to make America the envy of the ages. George Allen and I had a free-ranging discussion that extended beyond the time allocated for this meeting. We shared our respective thoughts and experiences about the kinds of issues that would engage a Virginia Secretary of Natural Resources with eight agencies to guide. It was important to him that the person he would choose for the post have an appreciation for his determination to focus on guiding State government policies and practices so that economic growth could improve the quality of life for Virginians.

He knew that the political context of environmental issues was difficult for conservatives in general and for Republicans in particular, because there existed something of a conventional wisdom—even among many conservatives and Republicans—that an improved economy and an improved environment were simply not compatible. The political Left and its handmaidens in the media had been successful over the past thirty years in creating that mindset. Allen instinctively sensed, and I knew perfectly well from my familiarity with the politics of environmental policy, that many people, particularly government and other elites, would agree with the statement: "The only way the environment can be protected is for government to closely regulate and harshly punish companies to keep polluters in line."

This view was even more dominant in Washington, a fact that would make it difficult for any governor to adopt sensible and balanced policies that improved the environment without needlessly harming a state's economy. For four years under George Bush, the Environmental Protection Agency had generally become more intrusive in its approach both to businesses and to state governments. In 1993, Bill Clinton and Albert Gore came to power, promising to accelerate this trend and sharpen, not ease, the effort to impose national environmental policies through the EPA. This made dealing with the agency a challenge for any state. The problem was especially acute for us, however, because we felt we had a mandate of our own, at least for Virginia, to pursue environmental improvements in a different way than the Gore-Clinton model.

While Allen didn't go into detail that November day about the coming fights that might or might not take place, he was realistic enough to know that there probably would be conflicts. So our discussion turned to ways in which his Governorship might contribute to his overall agenda for serving the people of Virginia while at the same time contributing to the correction of that prevailing conventional wisdom that presumed an ever-intrusive federal role in environmental regulation. We talked about the importance of guiding principles that would apply under these circumstances, and we explored the broad outlines of what I subsequently articulated as the principles that I would use to advance environmental policy for Virginia under my stewardship.

We agreed, for example, that excessive federal regulations are injurious to the principles of sound conservation management. It is in the nature of government, and even the environment, that decisions made close to the point of impact are likely to be the best. Yes, there are some phenomena that spill over into a neighboring state or district. For the most part, though, environmental concerns need not be homogenized and made into

4

policy at the federal level resulting in one-size-fits-all regulations and mandates.

We also shared a belief that people are actually an important "natural" resource—and, in fact, their ingenuity and creativity, and their basic and native environmentalism, are indeed the most important resource of all. If government could tap into this genius, it could solve virtually all environmental problems, as scientific advances, new products and production methods, and the incessant drive to do a better job with fewer resources come into play. In fact, most of the great pollution control devices and advances of the last 25 years have come as a result of new products and devices developed by private industry, from industrial stack-scrubbers to new benign cleaning methods for microchip production. Of course, some of these innovations would never likely have been developed were it not for tax, regulatory, and other pressures and incentives to produce them. But it is equally true that when presented with the right incentives the market responded, and fairly rapidly at that. Allen and I both shared this populist optimism about people and companies moving in the right direction if they are encouraged—and the accompanying belief that they need not be whipped and bullied into being good individual or corporate citizens.

In a political sense, our approach to the environment started from the assumption that environmentalism has won a place in the pantheon of public virtues. George Allen believed, and I shared that belief, that taking care of our air, water, and other natural resources is something the vast majority of Americans support and, indeed, insist upon.

We also agreed on where we parted company with some of the extreme groups and activists that would, in effect, form our loyal, but intensely critical opposition in Virginia. We thought, for example, that environmental efforts should focus on the environment, as paradoxical as that may sound. For too many groups, the more pressing goal seems to have become one of handing out the maximum number of fines or penalties, as if this equaled a better natural resource base for our children.

We also agreed that environmental policy should be based on real science, and that scientific findings, by their very nature, should be open to interpretation by other scientists and to the people. For our opponents, the inclination seemed to be to declare a disaster or the threat of a disaster first, and then do their homework. This not only leads to occasional unnecessary panics and anxiety for the people, but in many cases, actually harms the environment.

In short, our vision for Virginia's environmental policy was to focus on caring for the quality of the resources, rather than to use the public's genuine concern about the environment as a tool to hammer one's political opponents.

Governor-elect Allen, I felt at the time, shared my understanding that fighting pollution and red tape might not win us any friends with the federal EPA or among extremist groups. Yet he was determined to approach the issue in a civil way—to fight against the ideas and policies of our opponents, but without impugning their motives. I also approached the issue that way, too.

Finally, we thought that the government should be held to the same standards of behavior, if not higher ones, than those it imposes on its own citizens and private enterprises. It is embarrassing and aggravating to contemplate that the largest polluter in the United States is the federal government—followed, in most parts of the country, by state and local governments. Part of this is a function of government's mere size—itself a commentary—but part of it reflects the arrogance and cynicism of some elected officials.

What stays with me long after that talk about principles and ideas is a vivid picture of Allen and his obvious human quality—his sincere personal concern for the environment. Here was a man, for example, who on a first date, took his future wife canoeing. He reacted with pride and excitement later in the Administration at reports that the population of bald eagles was increasing in Virginia. Allen was a hunter, and defended hunting as a natural and appropriate sport whenever challenged. But he believed in an ethic of hunting, such as making use of whatever game was killed so that hunting was not a mere vain sport. Allen was greatly offended by hunters who took their game only as a trophy, wasting the meat and coat and other products. Out of this sincere concern for animal husbandry, Allen volunteered time every year to speak out and actively support with his own contributions Hunters for the Hungry, a group of hunters who processed deer meat and provided food from the donations of Virginia hunters to homeless shelters, orphanages, and other charitable groups.

After that talk, I felt I had met a kindred spirit in George Allen. I still had no strong expectation, though, that I was likely to be headed to Richmond. That low level of expectation solidified as the Thanksgiving holiday passed, then one week in December, and then another.

It was to my surprise, then—but my happy surprise—that late on the afternoon of December 17, an assistant came in to tell me that I had a telephone call "from someone claiming to be Governor-elect Allen."

It was the Governor-elect and he had called to ask me to join his Cabinet. I accepted, honored to be asked and privileged to serve my adopted state. As we wrapped up the conversation, he asked me to stand by for a call from Betsy Beamer with details on the next action for me. I agreed but told him that I had to be on my way shortly as my husband and I celebrated our wedding anniversary every month, a tradition we had started when we first married to assure that we would keep our priorities straight. He laughed, told me what a romantic idea that was, and he would keep that Dunlop tradition a secret if I would. Betsy Beamer's call came within minutes and I made my "anniversary dinner" with my husband on time that evening and every month during the four years I served in Richmond.

Inauguration day was frigid. Virginians, used to an occasional cold snap but not to a Midwestern-style freeze, wrapped up as best they could, drew up their coats, and breathed mist. The weather was a metaphor for what was about to happen to the Richmond political class, which, after 20 years of warm, comfortable, good-ol'-boy political control of Virginia government, was about to get a bracing slap in the face.

I had seen Ronald Reagan's inaugurations in 1980 and 1984, but from more of a distance. The inauguration of a new state administration is, of course, more intimate. And, for me, as a member of the cabinet, Governor Allen's swearing-in had special meaning.

No sooner had George Allen taken that oath to become Virginia's sixty-seventh governor, than he threw down something of a gauntlet. Political science professors sometimes associate conservatism with a tired elitism that looks mainly to preserve existing arrangements and privileges. That is some people's definition of the term, but it was never mine, and it was certainly not George Allen's. Unlike too many office holders—and there are some in both parties—Allen made it clear he was not becoming governor merely to hold office or enjoy the perks and attentions that come with it. He was in office to change policy and improve people's lives.

Allen promised to work "for you, the people of Virginia—not for the stolid, status quo, monarchical elitists." The stolid, status quo, monarchical elitists, mostly now just grumpy old men and their handmaidens, sitting behind him glowered. He pledged to wage war against "pesky bureaucrats" on all fronts, and to remove "the heavy, grimy boot of excessive taxation and spending and regulation" that stood in the way of progress and opportunity in Virginia. He put on notice the political class in Richmond and Washington "that has lost touch with the people."

"Whenever the rights and prerogatives of Virginia are threatened by Washington," he continued, "I will stand up to fight the beast of tyranny and oppression that our federal government has become."

Many in the crowd heard only a rousing address appealing to Virginia values and aspirations. I was hearing marching orders, and an energizing start to the Administration.

My first deed as a Secretary-designate, in December 1993, was to be introduced at a press conference. Characteristically, George Allen minced no words in making his intentions to steer a decisive course. "Environmental conservation and historic preservation are, and will remain, critical to the quality of life of all Virginians," he told the reporters. "But concern for the environment should not come at the expense of people, their property, and jobs." It was no coincidence that Allen announced my appointment in tandem with his selection for Commerce Secretary. His administration would be "equally, if not more, concerned about jobs" than regulation, he said. Virginians could expect his new environmental secretary to be "reasonable on regulations; she realizes that property rights are important in our Constitution."

It was my turn at the podium. "Governor, I share your conviction that our most important natural resources are the people of this great Commonwealth," I said. "It is a well-documented fact that a growing economy results in an improving environment. I want to help ensure that individuals and families have the wherewithal and opportunities to better the environment in which we live."

For the opportunity about to unfold I also gave "thanks and praise to my heavenly Father who has provided abundantly in my life and is the Creator of this beautiful state, which I love, and for which I shall soon bear significant responsibility for good stewardship."

Allen opened the floor for questions. Don Baker of *The Washington Post* was first. "How old are you?" he asked me.

"A gentleman never asks such a question of a lady," I said.

"I'm not a gentleman," he retorted. The other reporters chuckled, and I did too. Even though I didn't usually agree with *The Washington Post's* reports on our policies, I generally started out a new relationship with a *Post* reporter from a position of respect. Baker had his own point of view, and perhaps he really wasn't a gentleman.

The second question was directed to Allen, though it felt like an attempt to belittle my religious convictions or dismiss me. "Was Mrs. Dunlop's appointment a pay-off to the Christian Right?"

"Becky is a pay-off to the citizens of Virginia," Allen said defiantly, with a characteristic twinkle in his bright blue eyes.

My loyalty toward him swelled. I had not expected such craven hostility from the press before I even took office, but I also had not expected Allen's valiant, reflexive support.

In retrospect, that initial press conference defined our relationship. For the next four years, I would be hammered relentlessly by people who relished partisan combat and who thought they could make political hay and undermine Governor Allen's approach to improving the environment by attacking me.

Allen's support never wavered. Never.

2. The California car

On January 17, 1994, an earthquake measuring 6.8 on the Richter scale jarred Northridge, California, leaving 61 people dead and more than 11,000 wounded. Structural losses, including damage to the area's extensive freeway system, were estimated at $13 billion. Televised pictures of the tragedy played over several days, reinforcing the human impact of the disaster.

To these suffering Californians, though, an arcane statute brought relief. Section 404 of the Emergency Supplemental Appropriations Act of 1994 requires the General Accounting Office to report to Congress on federal laws, unfunded mandates, and regulatory requirements likely to impede recovery from national disaster.

California officials told federal investigators it would be virtually impossible to remove and demolish earthquake debris without violating the Clean Air Act. The National Environmental Policy Act, which requires environmental impact studies before construction can commence, would slow the rebuilding of highways. Abiding by the Clean Air Act was difficult for California under the best of circumstances. Now it would be virtually impossible. Additionally, the state was scheduled to begin federally mandated sales of low-emission vehicles—"the California car" powered by specially refined made-to-order gasoline—that was supposed to produce less than half the emissions of present cars by the end of 1998.

"The only way you could really meet that, unless you wanted to consider sails or rubber bands," said Kelly Brown of Ford Motor Company, "was with an electric vehicle of some sort." But engineers had yet to develop a practical model. Researchers in California laboratories were frantically trying to develop fuel cells, gas and electric hybrids, and better battery-powered cars.

Scientists and engineers, though, said it was unreasonable to expect them to have a practical and affordable product within five years—especially now that their talents were needed to help rebuild the state.

EPA Administrator Carol Browner faced political reality. California had 54 electoral votes. It was the keystone of the coalition her long-time boss, Al Gore, hoped to build should he decide to run for president in the year 2000. Browner agreed to relax the state's compliance schedule, including the imposition of the California car.

The agency and its defenders undoubtedly would tout that as a testament to flexibility. What it really showed me is how arbitrary the EPA is in applying its standards, and how very political the Clinton-Gore Administration was in its application of the laws.

Were an airline burdened with additional costs brought on by natural disaster, the Federal Aviation Administration hardly would permit skimping on safety regulations. Nor would the Food and Drug Administration throw a bone to farmers and food processors by relaxing health standards on edibles. If either agency rescinded its rules, people could become sick or die. Likewise, when the EPA announces and sets standards, its officials commonly say that nothing less than tens of thousands of lives are literally at stake—a claim Administration officials made repeatedly in the case of clear air standards, at least when it suited them. So why was it, I wondered, that by relaxing the standards now—when it suited them—left them any less guilty of being "callous towards human life?"

In the specific instance, of course, I agreed with the EPA's decision—but only because the standards were not essential to public health to begin with. That the EPA could do so demonstrates that the rules themselves reflect little more than bureaucratic caprice and mission creep. Little wonder so many people suspect the persistent press to make government standards ever less tolerant is less a calculation to protect the environment than to protect 20,000 EPA jobs and advance a "one-size-fits-all" command and control economy.

The EPA's decision to waive standards and sanctions in the wake of the Los Angeles area earthquake was one of its first major actions during my tenure in Virginia. If I was skeptical of the agency's actions during the ensuing four years, it was, as far as I could see, based on hard experience.

Neither the relaxation of clean-up rules after the 1994 quake, nor the decision not to immediately impose special electric automobile fleet requirements, produced the kind of further disaster that some politicians like to predict. In fact, Los Angeles air quality, while still virtually the worst in the nation, continued improving after 1994.

A s the earthquake did its horrible damage to Southern California, my own first seismic confrontation with the EPA was only a few weeks away. In February of 1994, the Ozone Transport Commission (OTC) met to discuss which of several hypothetical choices for improving air quality we would accept from EPA. The commission, a regional government panel comprised mainly of secretaries for natural resources or environment from 12 Northeastern states and the District of Columbia—consisting almost entirely of appointed officials—had to agree on a strategy that would help reduce air pollution in our region.

I say "hypothetical choices" because, while on paper the states could choose between various methods in devising their State Implementation Plans, or SIPs, in practical terms they could not. The EPA always had a favored option that it hoped would be picked "freely," but it was prepared to apply threats and sanctions if its wished-for choice were not honored. If the states did "the right thing" and picked the EPA option on our own, then we would have the burden of explaining the sacrifices associated with it to our citizens. If we didn't, the EPA officials would denounce us as anti-environment and press for the policy they wanted. Then they would ram it down our throats anyway, and tell people they had reluctantly been forced to impose it on recalcitrant state officials. A colleague of mine likened these meetings and SIPs to an ice-cream vendor offering any of 31 flavors—and we in the states could have whatever we wanted, as long as it was chocolate.

The flavor the EPA clearly wanted the Northeastern states to freely choose was some form of mandatory sales of the California car (minus the specially formulated gasoline that was a key element for it to run most efficiently) and electric vehicles.

January's snows were becoming February's slush as we convened at the Shoreham Hotel, a posh Washington mainstay that had hosted inaugural balls for every President since Franklin Roosevelt. Jack Kennedy courted Jacqueline Bouvier in the hotel's Blue Room in the 1950s.

These meetings and others like them always made me a bit uncomfortable. The surroundings didn't fit the model of government budgetary austerity that both parties have been proclaiming as a necessity since the 1970s. It was a little too much like one of those World Bank or International Monetary Fund affairs where aloof international bureaucrats and Third World dictators hobnob over caviar and champagne while discussing the tragedy of African poverty.

We filed into a lush hotel ballroom and seated ourselves at a U-shaped table, each state official behind an identifying placard. As this was my first such meeting, I watched curiously as the others filed in, trying to match faces to names and names to states. In general, my initial impression was that the other state officials were less conservative than me, and this was true, although as time went on, I forged friendly relationships with both Democrats and Republicans. In my experience, the typical state environmental official, at least in our part of the U.S., thought of himself or herself as a common-sense moderate, and was one. There were a few zealots, but for the most part, these were people trying to make the air and water in their states cleaner. It is a telling fact that such a group of people would find themselves in frequent conflict with the federal Environmental Protection Agency.

Mary Nichols, assistant administrator for air, represented the EPA. She was cordial to me and I was to her, although it was clear from this first meeting that we were likely to have our disagreements in the months and years to come.

Arthur Davis, the chairman of the commission, welcomed New Jersey's Robert Shinn and me, the two new members of the commission representing newly elected governors. Neither of us was intimidated by our status as novices to this group. (My counterpart, Secretary of Transportation Robert Martinez, was also appointed to the OTC by Governor Allen as each state had two representatives and alternates but secretary Martinez did not attend this meeting.)

Shinn immediately proposed the Commission delay for up to one year its vote on imposing the California car. Connecticut's Timothy Keeney said that would put the states at jeopardy: The states needed approval for the details of the California car proposition from the EPA in time to submit their state plans to EPA in November. Without these being submitted and accepted, states faced possible EPA sanctions for non-compliance with the regulations drawn up under the Clean Air Act. In English, that meant a paperwork deadline must be met regardless of whether or not the action outlined in the paperwork had any real impact that would benefit the environment. If the paperwork deadline was not met, EPA had authority under Section 179 of the Clean Air Act to impose stiff penalties.[1] Shinn was not deterred.

---

[1] Section 179 of the Clean Air Act gives EPA broad authority to impose sanctions on states which fail to comply with EPA's clean air regulation. In this context, EPA allows itself great latitude. For example EPA can find a state implementation plan insufficient or incomplete or not timely as defined by the federal agency. Sanctions can be imposed in the non-attainment areas or, at EPA's discretion, statewide. These sanctions would begin with stationary sources (manufacturing industry, utilities, etc.) with two to one offset requirements for new or modified sources. Let's say that DuPont wanted to expand its operation in Richmond and asked for a permit to increase its NOx emissions by 4 tons. To get a permit, the company would have to reduce emissions elsewhere by 8 tons. Such restrictions would discourage new industries from coming to Richmond and to other non-attainment or

"In New Jersey's opinion," he went on, "the recommendation is premature." Recent studies, such as the New Jersey Institute of Technology's analysis of environmental impact and cost, had raised critical questions about the efficiency of the California car. Those ought to be answered before the Commission proceeded with a recommendation to impose a vehicle on the public that would not work, Shinn said—and he was right. But when the chairman finally put the issue to a vote, the motion to delay was defeated. Only New Hampshire and Virginia supported Shinn's suggestion that the panel consider new data.

The floor was returned to Connecticut's Keeney, who moved to adopt and forward his resolution. The states comprising the Ozone Transport Region face a pervasive ozone non-attainment problem, he argued. The resolution called for a policy that, with the 1999 model year, no corporation, person, or other entity would be able to sell, import, deliver, purchase, lease, receive, or register a new passenger car or light-weight truck that did not conform to the emission characteristics of the California car. If the majority of states agreed, he continued, the recommendation would be sent to the EPA, which would have nine months to consider granting approval of this extraordinary government *diktat*.

The first thought that flooded into my mind was, "Oh, my goodness, Al Gore wasn't kidding about wanting to eliminate the internal combustion engine and these people are his shock troops! Do their Governors and citizens know about this?" But I didn't say that.

Instead, I stood up to voice my concern about what seemed to me to be a vast over-reaction to circumstance.

---

maintenance areas in Virginia until EPA determined that the state adequately complied with the regulation and demonstrated its compliance by submitting an acceptable SIP. As well, six months after the imposition of the stationary source sanctions, EPA would impose transportation sanctions preventing the state from advancing most transportation projects other than safety and mass transit. This would give EPA the power to paralyze a state's commercial shipping and with it, much of the economy.

"Virginia will vote against the motion today for several reasons," I began. "The first is timing. Governor Allen has been in office for less than two weeks....This is not really enough time to evaluate the different versions of the recommendation that are being made nor to review the supporting studies that evaluate the science and the practical impacts on Virginia and the nation."

"Second, and perhaps most important," I continued, "Governor Allen has made it clear that he is opposed to unfunded federal mandates—and federal mandates in general." So far, Virginia had a principled reason to oppose this action, and a scientific one.

Virginia also had a special problem with the scheme, I pointed out. Only the northern portion of the state was included in the Ozone Transport Region. It was easy to predict that if "no corporation, person, or other entity shall sell, import, deliver, purchase, lease, rent, acquire, receive, or register" a new passenger car or light-weight truck that does not conform to the emission characteristics of the California car, then Northern Virginia would have incredible difficulties from a logistical standpoint. There is a large transient population with military personnel, federal employees, and political and congressional appointees moving in and out of the area continuously. Would the EPA want to exempt them from the mandate to purchase and drive these new expensive vehicles? (It normally did: As I was to find in office, the federal government often did not behave by the standards it set for others.) If so, would that be fair application of the law?

There were other practical problems that I urged my fellow commissioners to consider. "What about Northern Virginia car dealers with locations elsewhere in our state?" I asked. Was the EPA intent that they should maintain two distinct inventories that could not be exchanged? Indeed, that is exactly what the EPA mandate would require, and everyone present knew it. The Virginia automobile dealers would need to become engaged in this battle, I thought. What about the federal government's fleet of vehicles? Federal agencies were not meeting the current standards for air emissions. Did EPA intend to exempt the federal government from compliance with its new rules, as is so often the case? Not one of the OTC commissioners cared to speculate about that.

Finally, I asked, would not mandating this new, more expensive car surely slow overall fleet turnover, discouraging everyone, but especially lower income families and fixed income seniors, from trading in older vehicles that were more likely to pollute for newer, more technologically advanced and less polluting models?

As incredible as it sounds, I had the feeling I was the first person ever to raise such common-sense concerns in this OTC group. I was a bit concerned, as I spoke, that perhaps I was speaking out too boldly for someone new on this job, but my primary job was to look after Virginia's environment and citizens. Later, after getting a few words of encouragement, and as I worked more with the commission and those who followed its activities over the next four years, I came to realize that some of my colleagues and many of the observers were relieved that someone had brought up these points. Many of them had been thinking along similar lines, but hoping against hope that someone else would take the lead in opposing some of the decisions shoved down on us from Washington—leaving us with a sane policy, but enabling them to escape Carol Browner's considerable political wrath.

Sensing a little bit of this concern even among a new group of colleagues, I closed with an appeal to them and their respective state's sense of self-worth. I encouraged them to think of themselves, and their voters, as competent people capable of making sound judgments without mandates from appointed officials in Washington.

"Virginia believes in federalism and the spirit of federalism—that states should be laboratories for testing ideas that will achieve the goal of our country and the goal of our region, which is cleaner air for our citizens," I said, hoping to sway the other commissioners. "Virginia encourages the other OTC states

18

to vote *no* on this decision today, and hopes you will understand why Virginia has made this decision."

I had at least one ally. Christopher Tulou of Delaware said his state also would be voting no, based on the problem of timing. The Commission, he noted, was being asked to make a "very fundamental decision" at a time when there were many "substantive concerns still floating around" about the efficacy of a California Low Emission Vehicle or FedLEV proposal.

Others emerged, too. State legislators from several of the affected states contacted me and my staff echoing Tulou's concerns—and ours—that a lot of substantive concerns remained.

Indeed there were a lot of substantive concerns remaining. Parts of California had the worst air quality in the nation, often caused by unique geographical and weather conditions. The Northeast did not share its problems. Los Angeles in particular suffered from levels of smog and particulate matter not seen in most of the United States. Requiring northeastern states to take the California cure was like treating the common cold with chemotherapy.

It seemed clear to me that the EPA was eager, almost desperate to force other states to adopt what would otherwise be a gross and obvious imposition on a single state. Forcing demand for the California car and electric vehicles to other states would spread the economic cost over a broader area, and appeal to the automakers as well. Few things are as expensive in industry in terms of unit cost as producing a small number of a highly specialized item—as the Pentagon learned in the 1980s when it ordered defense contractors to produce only ten copies of a huge plexiglass toilet seat cover for a long-range bomber, yielding the infamous (if inaccurately named) "$750 toilet seat." This was part of the economic and political problem with producing 10,000 or even 100,000 special cars for California. Imposing the car on the Northeast would also spread the political burden, removing the impression that the EPA was singling out California—and indeed, for the most part, Southern California—for special "treatment."

Nichols, I noticed, seemed to cringe even at the term "California car," and always preferred one of the bureaucratic acronyms such as "LEV," the federal acronym for Low Emission Vehicle.

Of course, *all* new cars sold in all of the United States already qualified as low-emission vehicles. The latest models pollute between 90 percent and 97 percent less, depending on the car and the pollutant, than cars made in the 1960s, as Eric Peters later noted in *The Washington Times*. Air quality was improving because new cars burned cleaner, and it would get even better as more people traded in out-of-tune, ill-maintained clunkers for more pristine and technologically advanced models. Mandating elaborate combustion and exhaust systems that inevitably would raise sticker prices would only delay that progress.

Tulou reminded commissioners that automakers also had a proposal on the table, *i.e.*, that they be given the time to develop a reasonable alternative to the so-called California car. Delaware would not endorse the Connecticut proposal, he said, because "there is the potential that some alternative that is as effective as the California proposal that [the commission] otherwise would endorse could be put in place for the region."

None of that mattered to Maryland's representative, who seemed intoxicated by the workings of government and of rash vows. The "petition process gives the OTC both challenge and opportunity," he waxed rhapsodic. "It also allows us to work collaboratively with the commission, the states, industry, and the EPA and to formally engage and redefine the collaborative process with EPA..." To him, the goal was to "press technology so that we, in fact, can have an affordable and workable" low-emission vehicle. Therefore Maryland would be enthusiastically supporting this petition and, he implied, any others like it that came its way.

Trudy Coxe of Massachusetts said she "didn't want to commend anyone for fear of leaving somebody out." Like the Maryland representative, she too hoped to "press technology," but at least Coxe was not hypocritical. She said she drove an electric car and told us how much she liked it. Even though I disagreed with Coxe on many issues, I felt a certain liking for her and gave her greater respect from that moment on. I admire political leaders who put their money and their lifestyle where their mouth is—as opposed to the limousine liberals who bash school vouchers, but then drive their kids to private schools in SUVs. Who knows? Maybe someday policy activists and elites living by the standards they set will become the rule, I mused.

Coxe also announced that she had spent a day with doctors and patients and had seen people suffering from serious health issues. Not having witnessed the same horrors, she said, the rest of us might find it "very hard to appreciate how important our work is and how important it is for all of us within this region to work as closely as we possibly can," she explained. Surprising no one, Coxe announced that Massachusetts would vote *yes.* It was a purely emotional appeal, but it was effective.

This is a real problem for those fighting for a sane environmental policy: It is difficult to uphold science in the face of such "human suffering" appeals. It is also, however, a duty in my book, because if we enact policies that aren't based on the scientific facts, we don't reduce the kind of suffering Commissioner Coxe was talking about—we actually increase it.

All this moralistic mastery was a tough act for New Jersey's Shinn to follow, but he did. "There is no question that air quality is vitally important to the health of our citizens and the economic viability of the region," he conceded, "but many significant questions remain." Again, Shinn tried to persuade the holdouts to let facts intrude on an emotional judgment, pointing out that three recent studies had raised important questions about the value of the California cars. New Jersey's Institute of Technology had concluded that "insufficient data now exist to determine whether the California car will achieve expected pollution reductions." Researchers at Johns Hopkins had concluded "that the benefits of the California program for the Northeast are unlikely to be achieved in the time frame required by the Clean Air

Act." The Johns Hopkins team also reported that requiring the California car without California reformulated gasoline"—as the commission in fact proposed—"may not produce the needed results."

Most crucial were preliminary findings of the EPA's own internal studies. Administrator Browner's own scientists had determined, as Shinn reported, that "electric vehicles may cause higher overall pollution levels than the gasoline-powered vehicles they are designed to replace when emissions from power plants are considered." Agency researchers had determined that the factories would produce enough pollution—particularly while generating the power to charge the cars' batteries—to offset any reductions in car emissions. When I heard Shinn describe these findings, I was a bit stunned. What other information did Carol Browner have that might argue against the very policy she was pushing?

In fact, as we learned later, the EPA was keeping to itself several little secrets it knew about "clean cars." In 100 miles of driving, for example, an electric car running on a lead-acid battery releases about 393 grams of carbon monoxide per mile—roughly 10 percent more than the 354 grams a gasoline-powered car generates. Disposal of the spent batteries presented another challenge. Their lead-acid and nickel-hydride content likely would qualify as hazardous waste, making old car batteries potentially as much of a waste-disposal headache as used tires, at least in the near term. This did not make the idea of electric cars bad, just not an ideal alternative for EPA to be mandating in 1994.

Indeed, these factors raised another question no one seemed prepared to answer. So-called zero-emissions cars, even when developed, were going to have sticker prices far above what most people could pay. When the battery-powered Ford Ecostar became available on the market, after 5 years of further development, the base list price was $100,000 for a two-year lease. Who was going to buy them? It was one thing for the government to mandate production, quite another to mandate purchases. Inevitably, the high-priced cars would be subsidized, raising sticker prices on every model. This would exacerbate yet another familiar problem:

People would hold onto older cars, produced at a time when the standards were lower and combustion technology was not as advanced, longer. Those who did hold onto the older cars would be adding to, not subtracting from, the amount of pollution in the air: Newer cars tend to pollute less, at least when they are designed by automakers and not by government committees.

"We in New Jersey are committed to improving our air quality, but we are committed to do so in a responsible manner with thorough information to make an informed decision," Shinn concluded. "New Jersey is not opposing adoption of the Low Emission Vehicle in New Jersey when a complete analysis shows this approach to be appropriate," he explained, "but right now New Jersey believes that there is not enough information to proceed."

Shinn's cogent analysis, unfortunately, went unheeded at this meeting. Keeney recommended a roll-call vote. Eschewing logic, evidence, and timeliness—in my opinion—the commission voted 9-4 in favor of "asking" the EPA to require California standards for emission equipment on new cars sold in the Northeast after 1998, but not the specially formulated gasoline that they were designed to burn. As well, the commissioners asked that states be permitted to mandate zero-emission cars, which would require subsidies estimated to raise the costs on all new cars by $700 to $2,000. Only Delaware, New Hampshire, New Jersey, and Virginia voted against the plan that cold ominous day. Of course, the Commission was "asking" EPA to do what EPA would otherwise try to mandate entirely on its own even to the extent of imposing all kinds of sanctions on states that refuse to comply. This was truly phony federalism

Even so, I saw a ray of hope in the proceedings—indeed, more than a ray. First of all, in voting for a special vehicle without the special fuel requirements needed to make it burn cleaner, the administrators were mainly showing that they wanted to have their cake and eat it, too. At some point in the future, we would in all likelihood make a rational decision to follow this policy to its logical conclusion—or turn back.

Furthermore, although we had lost a 9-4 vote, the two major leaders of the minority (Mr. Shinn and I) were brand new on the job. We would have to marshal our facts and persuade some of our moderate colleagues, but this is democratic politics. However they had voted, some of the administrators appeared to be open to facts and reason. If nothing else, Shinn and I had showed some of our more cautious friends that the Emperor should be questioned—and can be questioned. This was to prove valuable on this and other issues.

When the time came for EPA to talk, the chairman proceeded to introduce Mary Nichols, who said the agency recognized what an important obligation it had to implement policies in collaboration with the states. She was glad to see, she said, the spirit of cooperation and looked forward to the states moving ahead on the plan they were choosing. The other panelists and I remained straight-faced during her pronouncement. We all knew, though, that if the EPA thought up something more onerous, it would impose another freely-chosen plan. I smiled to myself, though, because I was convinced this was not the end of the issue.

The OTC's vote meant that cars would be built to fulfill direct government edicts instead of consumer demands—arguably, Gore's and Browner's ultimate goal. "Obviously, it makes little sense for each of us to burn up all the energy necessary to travel with several thousand pounds of metal wherever we go," Gore said. The vice president dreamed of Americans tooling around in little more than souped-up golf carts, if that. But he realized that this will happen only through government coercion.

No sooner did the commission and EPA reach a decision, however, than the states were confronted with the realities of trying to implement it. This created an opening for getting back to some kind of reasonability, and I was determined to make use of this opportunity to correct what I saw as a dangerous boondoggle.

As carmakers tried explaining to the EPA, the technology for electric cars was not perfected. Manufacturers had been unable to develop a battery that could last more than 70 miles. If the driver used his windshield wipers, heater, air conditioner, or radio, the battery's life was reduced still more. How were commuters in the Northeast going to like it when they had to drive to work in below-freezing weather and couldn't run the heater without draining the battery? Suppose, while the car was plugged in for overnight recharging, one of the kids needed to go to an emergency room? Families owning electric cars essentially would be without transportation for much of the day.

Even environmental activist groups sometimes conceded that electric cars weren't necessarily the best strategy for reducing pollution in the Northeast. Some mused about eliminating hair dryers, or even home refrigerators as an alternative. The EPA's Nichols was too politic to say something that frank, but she, too, dismissed the automakers' protests. Compelling manufacturers to make electric cars was "like creating a pot of money that someone is going to get," Nichols said. "Someone is going to be the winner of a very big prize, which is going to be 2 percent of the California new motor vehicle market in 1998."

When I read these remarks of Nichols, I smiled to myself. Nichols had fought for years against the efforts of auto manufacturers to include the costs of pollution-control equipment in window-sticker prices. If consumers were willing to put part of their own paychecks into creating this "pot of money," why did Nichols bitterly oppose letting them know how much they were putting in?

The Nichols attitude particularly rankled me because I knew the agency rejected improvements in its regulatory scheme that could jeopardize its stronghold on industry. For instance, one company had developed a means of color-coding plant air emissions—say, red for Dupont, green for Monsanto, mauve for General Motors. (The actual method was even more sophisticated, involving creating a distinctive "signature" for different plants using specific chemicals.) But the EPA was not interested in the ability to track and penalize specific wrongdoers because then it couldn't justify exercising tight control over *all* businesses. Controlling pollution was less important than maintaining control itself.

It struck me that someone ought to at least listen to the automakers. Yes, they are a special interest, but they are also patriotic Americans—no less so, I would insist, than most of the environmental special interests who lobbied tirelessly for their own agenda. And they know something about making cars.

The car manufacturers told me there was a sensible middle ground. They believed they could build a lower-emissions car if they were not compelled to waste their time and resources trying to perfect an impractical electric model. The cleaner car would still burn gas, but would have lower emissions than the current models. It would be suitable for sale everywhere except California, where the standards were even more stringent and a specially reformulated gasoline was necessary to achieve the results the state and EPA were demanding.

The automakers' concept of the alternative of a "49-state car" made enormous sense to me. It presented me, however, with a philosophical dilemma. Was it fair to push a cleaner car for the entire nation, believing that mass marketing would hold down the price, when in fact the air quality problems caused by exceptional concentrations of automobile congestion are almost entirely localized, and site and situation specific? This is the kind of Hobson's choice so often confronting policy makers in public office dealing with deadlines and political logrolling.

I decided that Virginia should weigh-in behind the 49-state car. For one thing, it would improve air quality everywhere, and it would be phased in by beginning in the areas that experience more troublesome air quality issues. It would contribute significantly to avoiding days when the ground level ozone standard was exceeded in areas of heavily congested traffic. If auto manufacturers possessed practical technology to make a car that would produce less pollution—but not be significantly more expensive—then it made sense to market that car everywhere instead of just the Northeast. If one accepted the premise behind the formation of the OTC—that smog is a regional problem because it cannot be contained—then cars even marginally cleaner than those currently manufactured were advisable for more than 13 states.

Committed to these concepts, over the next few months I tried to rally support for the industry-standard 49-state car.

Virginia professional staff members Shawn King and Michael McKenna of DEQ and Ahmet Anday of DOT worked tirelessly to fashion a consensus. They represented Virginia at several round tables sponsored by EPA presumably to establish such a consensus among the states, auto manufacturers, oil companies, and environmental and health organizations. These seemed to be carefully orchestrated to create a forum to promote the OTC-California car LEV, not open discussions weighing the pros and cons of the two alternative plans. We all attended and facilitated many meetings in the Ozone Transport Region. Secretary Martinez worked with his transportation counterparts in the Ozone Transport Region and elsewhere in the country to keep them involved and knowledgeable about this decision that could affect transportation planning and state implementation plans so significantly. Each of us devoted many hours to this issue because the decision might well change Northern Virginia automobile standards beginning with 1999 models. We explained to other state leaders and to Governor Allen's own constituents that Virginia continued to support development of all kinds of new technology, including natural gas vehicles, electric vehicles, and especially hybrid vehicles.[2] But we did object, I said, to federal mandates and manipulation of the market.

At the next commission meeting—in Pittsburgh, in May 1994—chairman Arthur Davis of Pennsylvania noted that the automakers still were pressing to have their 49-state car proposal

---

[2] *Economic Growth and Improving Air Quality in Northern Virginia*, 1995.

reviewed. I was pleased that we were making some headway in the public debate, but their efforts seemed to be wearing thin with him. "If the manufacturers have something in addition to—beyond what has been put on the table with respect to how states can meet their statutory obligations," Davis said, "then obviously the commission would be interested in listening. If, however, this is a rehash of the kinds of discussions that have gone on up until now, there is no need to devote any additional time." He instructed Connecticut's Keeney to contact the manufacturers for assurance "that, in fact, there is something beyond what we have talked about thus far." Then he asked for discussions from members.

As Davis and the others might have predicted, I was the first to speak. Virginia enthusiastically supported hearing from the automakers, I told him. We were confident the other commissioners would appreciate such an opportunity. I offered to help in any way to facilitate the discussions that would focus on sound science and practical opportunities to improve air quality. How could it possibly harm us, I wondered, to have information? Certainly we had not been fully informed by the EPA, I thought—but I did not say this at the meeting.

It was an uphill battle. Carol Browner, who had been hand-picked for her job as head of the EPA by Gore, seemed intolerant of anything but the most radical proposals. To her, even the previous commission policy didn't go far enough. Whatever recommendations are developed, she said, had to do a better job of cleaning up the air than the plan proposed in the Northeast states' petition.

(Of course, in a sense, she was only pushing, from the opposite end of the spectrum, the illogic that I had seen in our recommendation of February. We disagreed on the way to improve that proposal, but clearly, imposing the California car on the Northeast, without requiring the specially reformulated gasoline that California had determined would make the car cleaner burning, was not an environmental proposal at all, but a compromise designed in committee that would do little or nothing to improve air quality in the Northeast.)

Browner shared Gore's philosophy that "Minor shifts in policy, marginal adjustments in ongoing programs, moderate improvements in laws and regulations, rhetoric offered in lieu of genuine change—these are all forms of appeasement, designed to satisfy the public's desire to believe that sacrifice, struggle, and a wrenching transformation of society will not be necessary."

At the May meeting and again in September, we took no decisive action on behalf of moving to a 49-state car policy. But I felt the ground was shifting. However much Mr. Gore and Ms. Browner might desire it, most of my colleagues were not looking to enforce a "wrenching transformation of society."

With only a few months to go before the commission's vote to require the California car was official, I received pleas from Virginia car dealers. They were, understandably, increasingly concerned.

"Adopting this regional plan would translate to more expensive new cars for customers in Virginia," wrote a car dealer from Bedford, "as incremental costs for natural gas and electric vehicles will be spread throughout our entire product line-up. Meanwhile, bordering states [some of which were not part of the OTC region at all] will not have this pricing adjustment." I told him I was sympathetic and doing what I could, even as it meant ruffling some of my colleagues in the other OTC states.

If environmental decisions were made in accordance with sound science the matter would have been settled in October, when an EPA analysis concluded that the 49-state car plan would achieve greater emission reductions than the EPA-OTC plan. We wrote Nichols a congratulatory message on the EPA's discovery. Certainly, we said, no objections remained to the proposal put forth by the automakers. Jason Vines of the American Automobile Manufacturers Associations wasn't so sure. He predicted, though, that "there's going to be a lot of public outrage if there's a plan that does as much or more than the California program…and at much less cost—and it's not at least looked at."

Perhaps it was at least looked at—but it didn't make any difference. Browner seemed almost defiantly indifferent to those of us urging her to be reasonable, practicable and thoughtful. I felt at the time that, perhaps, she was escalating her threats precisely because she was afraid she was losing ground; that she hoped to intimidate some of the states, which were beginning to move towards our position, into giving in to her as a matter of political support for the EPA even though they disagreed regarding policy. Events were about to strengthen that feeling.

In November 1994, Congressional Republicans engineered a political revolution of their own, taking control of the House of Representatives and the Senate for only the third two-year term since the Great Depression. Trent Lott became the new Senate Majority Leader. For the first time since I was an infant, the Speaker of the House was a Republican.

There is no question that the voting public had expressed its alarm at the overreaching of the Clinton-Gore Administration in so many ways—such as the administration's national health insurance plan—that mirrored what they were attempting to mandate with the California car and centralized emissions testing.

The impact the November elections had on EPA in its resistance to the 49-state care proposal was immediate. On December 14, Congressman Tom Bliley, soon to become chairman of the House Commerce Committee that has oversight over the EPA, wrote to Browner to "express several concerns." Had he been anyone other than a bow-tied Richmonder with gentility in his veins, he might have been more blunt. Even so, Bliley politely pointed out:

> Since the OTC submitted its petition in February, the domestic and foreign automobile manufacturers have proposed an alternative plan that would, *according to EPA*,

provide equal or better air-quality emissions reductions at lower cost and in a more timely manner than the OTC petition.

Furthermore, the automakers' proposal would provide air quality benefits for the entire country, not just for the northeast Ozone Transport Region.

I am concerned that the EPA will approve a program... not supported by the citizens and the legislatures of the affected jurisdictions. This must not happen, especially if a less intrusive compliance program is available.

Two days later, I wrote Browner with a similar request. "Two critical factors dictate that you should delay your decision," I urged. "First, representation on the OTC will be altered substantially due to the recent elections." Of course, I enjoyed writing that sentence, but I honestly would have made the same recommendation had the results been a Democratic sweep, "Secondly," as I and my colleagues had been urging all year, "a better alternative exists."

I pointed out that after the previous month's elections, seven of the 12 Northeastern states would have new governors, and the District of Columbia, a new mayor. "Next year, a substantial majority of the commission will not have been party to the vote to mandate California vehicles. The new members should be consulted and involved in the final resolution of this issue."

"Furthermore," I continued, "the extensive negotiations between the OTC states and the automobile manufacturers have brought substantial progress toward reaching an agreement on a 49-state car alternative, which is clearly superior... The 49-state car program will produce greater air quality improvement nationwide, and it avoids the economic harm which the OTC mandate would cause. It makes no sense now to discard suddenly this more effective, practical solution when we are so close to an agreement."

Although I never said it, it seemed clear to me one reason for the Democratic Party's stunning defeats in the November 1994 elections was the arrogance of Browner's regulatory agenda. Not her goal of clean air and water, which Governor Allen, I and

Republicans wanted too—but the almost monarchical way in which the Browner-Gore EPA issued its fiats, and the condescending way in which it dismissed requests for information, or a discussion of science, as ill-motivated lobbying by persons bent on destroying the ozone layer.

The Environmental Protection Agency wouldn't budge, though—or even take a time out. Instead of postponing her decision and taking time to re-assess both the scientific evidence and even the political power curve, Browner acted on impulse. Shortly after receiving my letter, Browner rejected the more effective 49-state plan, opting instead to impose expensive, unnecessary regulations on the Northeast. Even my staff, which had grown used to the tone and timing of Browner's instructions, was shocked to read the rather imperial document that arrived less than 100 hours after our request merely to think things over.

Carol Browner's decision, notably, came just days after Virginia had forced the EPA to back away from centralized emissions testing, a battle described in chapter three. One could safely assume the announcement was a means for the EPA to save face.

Looking back on it, it seems to me that Browner perhaps did take these matters personally. At best, she viewed them as a matter of raw power politics. I can honestly say that, from my point of view, they weren't. Governor Allen and I just sincerely disagreed with the EPA's methods to improve air quality—we felt there was a better way that cost less money and would reduce pollution just as effectively. (Remember, we were supported in this by the EPA's own analysis.) I had hoped that Carol Browner felt the same way. Reading her blast fax order to impose the California car, though, it certainly seemed like the fight now had to do more with raw muscle and face-saving than with any sincere policy concern.

Adding insult to the injury of phoney federalism, the Northeastern states were required to "ratify, within one year," the EPA's approval of their proposal, i.e., to accept our orders. Virginia had no intention of doing so, as I immediately made clear.

32

"Imposing this costly, unfunded mandate when a more cost-effective, practical solution exists is completely contrary to the election's resounding popular call for accountability and common sense in government," I said. "This move demonstrated once again that the EPA has utterly failed to heed the message that the voters sent to Washington in November."

Although this argument was more partisan than those I had pressed before, I felt it was only proper to acknowledge the will of American voters. The people had just enacted a sweeping makeover of leadership at the federal and many state levels. They wanted change. When President Clinton and Vice President Gore swept George Bush from the White House in 1992, they quite appropriately moved to implement parts of their agenda—succeeding in raising taxes, failing on national health insurance, and enacting compromises on other issues. Now there was a new mandate.

Interestingly, I noticed that elected Democrats, including President Clinton, moved quickly to take notice of the new landscape. Browner, for whatever reason, made it clear that she was not going to—and if anything, might be counted on to fight even more stubbornly.

In March, having failed to win a re-opening of the California car proposal before the commission and EPA, Attorney General James Gilmore, on behalf of the Commonwealth of Virginia filed a lawsuit against the EPA, accusing the agency of unlawfully usurping states' authority. While waiting for the case to wind its way through the courts, I continued to push for the 49-state car.

On March 11, 1997, the Allen-Gilmore-Dunlop efforts came to fruition. A three-judge panel of the U.S. Court of Appeals in Washington ruled that the EPA's behavior was illegal.

"[States'] independence signifies freedom from the dictates of a federal agency," wrote Judge Raymond Randolph on behalf of the unanimous court. If California cars are to be imposed on all unwilling states, then "the case must be made to Congress. EPA's rule does not respect the states' independent authority; it removes it."

I was gratified. I would have preferred that the EPA or the commission had responded to the logic of science. But if they would not, a court victory was the next best thing.

I took further satisfaction in knowing that, while the decision meant EPA and the commission couldn't impose a car policy on Virginia, nothing in that decision prevented states that wanted to do so from adopting electric vehicles or the California car for themselves. That states should be allowed to determine how they would meet standards had been our position all along, notwithstanding more than two years of vigorous opposition from the EPA. It felt good that our victory had protected Virginia's rights, but without taking any rights away from my colleagues or the citizens in Massachusetts, Pennsylvania, and other states.

Of the eight states and the District of Columbia that had fought to impose the California car on the Northeastern region, by the way, the number that ultimately adopted the California car for themselves was: Zero.

In August of 1997, Mary Nichols stepped down from her post as an assistant EPA administrator.

On her last day in office, Nichols was asked to cite the greatest accomplishments of her tenure.

Without a trace of irony, nor an ounce of shame, Nichols named the 49-state car plan, newly named the National Low Emission Vehicle, as one of her achievements.

3. Testing cars: EPA's Gosplan

In the spring of 1994, the federal government began threatening to cut off Virginia's share of federal highway funds. This time, the Environmental Protection Agency complained that automobile emissions testing in Northern Virginia was not sufficiently centralized. For years, Virginia had allowed drivers to go to any of several hundred filling stations or auto repair centers to have their car checked out for pollution. Now, EPA wanted us to adopt a system that would—in practice—mean there would be no more than 10-15 testing stations in all of Northern Virginia for the projected million cars and 500,000 annual tests.

As radical as the proposal was, I knew the agency was serious about such threats. I heard unconfirmed reports that Carol Browner wanted to "make an example" of Virginia. I didn't know whether she actually used this language. Whether she did or not, though, it was clear that her bureaucracy was treating us like an example. The people of my state, then, were to be a test case —singled out for punishment, in part, because some federal agency didn't like my politics. I could already picture the memorandum I'd receive if we didn't willingly serve as EPA's taxpayer test laboratory. I could also picture the long lines, 5-hour waits, blaring horns, and furious letters to the governor and me that would come if we did.

Even so, I could hardly believe what I was hearing as my staff and I met with EPA officials in July 1994, and listened to them explain why the new system was needed. What emerged was an expression of a profoundly low opinion of the people that live in Virginia—and, for that matter, the rest of the country. It always struck me that Browner, Gore, and their followers believed, in their hearts, that people aren't terribly smart or honest. But now, some of their top aides, including EPA Region III Administrator Peter Kostmayer, a former Member of Congress, were explicitly saying so.

To understand how anti-democratic the EPA's language sounded, it may help to review how emissions testing works in most places today, including my state—and then discuss how the agency insisted that we change this in Virginia.

If you're a driver in a state with any air quality problems, you probably have to take your car in once every couple years to make sure it isn't producing excess pollution. In many states, that's become a relatively painless process. Often it's done while you wait. The mechanic runs the engine, while a couple of relatively inexpensive machines measure the exhaust. And, in most cases you're off.

If you're not, the nice thing is, you're right at a service station. They can fix what's wrong. The mechanic runs the test again, and you're off. Only in a tiny percentage of cases do you even have to leave your car overnight.

After more than a decade, however, the agency was now refusing to accept this model.

Emissions testing at neighborhood service stations wouldn't work, the agency told us, because mechanics—eager to keep regular customers happy—would turn a blind eye to violators.

"What is this based on?" I asked, calm but dismayed. "Is there something that indicates Virginia stations are cheating or sloughing off?" This was not something raised to me before in any communication with EPA.

Kostmayer and his staff didn't answer directly—meaning that they had, in fact, no such evidence. They just said that it was "clear" that "there is a potential problem" with a system that was working in Virginia and elsewhere. EPA said its own study revealed that about half the stations in Virginia were not enforcing the law properly. As usual, however, the agency declined to document that claim.

The only way to avoid cheating, the EPA maintained, was to have government contractors test cars at separate, government-run sites. Those that failed would be required to go to private automobile repair centers or service stations for repairs. It sounded simple verbally. But note: As the mechanic who works on your car would not have the same testing equipment, the best he could do would be to guess what the problem was, and try to correct it.

The car then would go back to the original government site for retesting. What if it failed again? Well, you couldn't have it fixed there. You would just be at one of 10 or 15 test sites. Failing the test again, you'd have to return to the mechanic for more blindfolded repairs. What if you failed the test again? Tough luck. The mechanic fixing your car would keep working on it—or you'd try a new one. And the centralized testing agency would just keep testing your car, sending you back for repairs. No one would be responsible for fixing the problem—except for you. And you would continue to try until you had spent the $450 required by EPA which would qualify you for a waiver even if it did not repair your car.

Northern Virginia drivers, in other words, would be ping-pong balls in a game of bureaucratic table tennis. And, of course, this game would not clean the air. If anything, all the extra driving around and waiting in line and all the rest, would increase pollution from automobile emissions.

Further, EPA's whole emissions testing scheme was mandated to test newer cars, cars which pollute less than older cars. Older cars? For the most part, the oldest, most likely cars to pollute were exempted from testing, or given waivers under federal guidance.

As the state's Secretary of Natural Resources, I felt it was my responsibility to lead the resistance to this centralized government testing plan—the equivalent of the old 5-year "Gosplan" systems in the Soviet Union. I was facing off with the

Philadelphia-based Regional Director of EPA, Peter Kostmayer, a sincere and tenacious believer that because of popular resistance, special interests, and other forces, environmental policy needed to be made painful. We had known each other since I worked in Ronald Reagan's Interior Department and Kostmayer was a Democratic Congressman from Pennsylvania. Our relationship—though contentious—was cordial. Kostmayer reportedly appreciated that I was "always polite, always gracious," as he said, which "makes things easier"—up to a point. My stance on environmental issues continued to confound him.

I appreciated dealing with Kostmayer because he was a completely unrepentant big government, command and control, tax-and-spend liberal—and proud of it. There was no question about exactly where Kostmayer intended to take government policy—to Washington D.C., along with as many tax dollars and user fees as he could command. Unlike some of his persuasion, he was always most polite and civil to me personally.

In this instance, however, it wasn't easy to be gracious. I resented Kostmayer's implication that every other mechanic in Northern Virginia was a crook. No doubt, as in all businesses, there were a few chiselers. But it seemed far fairer to penalize cheaters than to penalize every car-owner in Northern Virginia. Through blind spot checks using government officials, it was quite possible to find and punish specific stations that were cheating, without running millions of innocent voters through the car-testing Gosplan mega-stations.

Moreover, Kostmayer's fears were demonstrably unfounded. A covert audit of Virginia service stations conducted the year before found 92 percent of them correctly executing major inspection procedures—far better than the EPA's claim of improper testing 50 percent of the time. Virginia was the only state in the nation requiring inspectors to attend courses in emissions technology—including classroom instruction and field certification—before obtaining a license. Kostmayer smiled. His approach seemed to be that Virginia drivers and mechanics were guilty until proven innocent.

38

"It ought to be assumed *a priori* that the states and the citizens will do the right thing," I protested. "The burden of proof ought to be placed squarely on EPA to demonstrate that a program is defective, its participants negligent, and its citizens accomplices in fraud." But that argument cut no ice with Kostmayer.

To allay the agency's fears, and to show the public we were going the extra mile, the emissions team at Virginia's Department of Environmental Quality (DEQ) developed an enhanced enforcement program. "Enhanced enforcement" is government-speak for putting more cops on the beat. Our plan would put into place more random and undercover inspections and stiffen the consequences of cheating. Certainly the likelihood of fraud would decline if prospective malefactors knew that such activity would incur stiff penalties.

Faced with such an unsettling proposal—one that effectively met his stated concern, but without adopting the car-testing Gosplan—Kostmayer suddenly reversed course. To my dismay, he now was arguing that service-station owners could not be trusted to test cars because they might *fail* cars falsely in order to profit from sham repairs. I had heard enough.

"It certainly is true there are bad actors in every line of business," I said. "But you're saying service station managers and mechanics in Northern Virginia are, by definition, cheats and thieves. You just don't trust service-station people."

Kostmayer was composed but condescending.

"That's true," he admitted coolly.

I understood what he was really saying: The EPA's faith was in government. Service-station operators could not be trusted because they were private citizens. This wasn't a fight about Virginia's air quality. It was fight about government control—whether Washington should dictate to states how to meet the requirements of the Clean Air Act.

Governor Allen and I vigorously opposed such intrusion. Kostmayer was equally dismayed by Virginia being "totally recalcitrant," as he saw it—"bordering on a kind of 19th century reactionary point of view." Kostmayer pretended never to understand that we weren't quibbling about whether the state must meet the federal air quality standards. We were asking only for flexibility in how to go about it—as the law allowed and in fact mandated. The Clean Air Act specifically required the EPA to "provide the states with continued reasonable flexibility to fashion effective, reasonable, and fair programs for the affected consumer." Yet to Kostmayer, the issue was simply whether or not Virginia could be made to "comply with the national standards."

More likely, the agency feared setting a dangerous precedent if one state got out of hand. The EPA was accustomed to being appeased, not to open rebellion. But they had underestimated George Allen—and me. he inclination to appease is entirely lacking from my behavioral repertoire when constitutional principles, sound science, and common sense are at stake. I felt no personal animus toward Kostmayer or his staff. But I saw no reason not to resist their centralized testing scheme.

When Governor Allen appointed me, one of my first actions had been to revoke Virginia's previous administration's plan for centralized emissions testing. Allen and I opposed EPA's strong-arming in principle. But were also opposed to such impracticality. Virginia's General Assembly had decided in 1993 that the money for building and operating emissions testing sites must come from revenue of the test's fee, which it capped at $8. But that would provide only enough money to build eight to 10 test sites in Northern Virginia—compared to the 375 garages then currently licensed to inspect and repair emissions systems—through which an estimated 1.2 million cars would have to pass bi-annually. Compelling citizens to drive miles out of their way, then sit and idle their engines in long lines while belching polluting fumes hardly seemed a rational method for improving air quality. It certainly was not a prescription for a successful program in an area where people already work long hours, often have long commutes and where many work for hourly wages.

Moreover, as I pointed out, simply building the test stations was not feasible. Where, in the crowded Washington suburbs that included the nation's priciest neighborhoods, were expanses of land able to accommodate 10-12 bay test stations drawing long lines of cars? What neighborhoods would want such disruptive activities in their midst? And, if they were not located in neighborhoods, we were back at the problem of distance from home and work and time spent commuting to the test station.

The most maddening aspect of the EPA's edict was that it would impose all that inconvenience on people for no real gain. The fact is, that by this late date in the auto emissions crusade, auto manufacturers had already wrung 90 to 97 percent of pollutants from emissions since clean-air laws first went into effect three decades earlier. Furthermore, auto manufacturers were constantly improving the performance of vehicles using computer miniaturization and other technology breakthroughs having nothing to do with government mandates.

Directly considering the issue at hand, the Rand Corporation had studied the comparative efficacy of test-only versus test-and-repair sites. "Based on effectiveness in reducing emissions," the study concluded, "we find no empirical evidence to require the separation of test and repair. Our research also indicates that a decentralized system, safeguarded with rigorous state supervisions, can be highly effective."

The General Accounting Office, a joint arm of the then-Democratic Congress and the Democratic Administration, warned EPA that its directive not only was insupportable, but likely to be counterproductive. EPA's program for more stringent emissions testing might not achieve the reduction envisioned, GAO warned, because of the behavioral response of motorists to higher costs and greater inconvenience.

The EPA claimed that an internal investigation had revealed substantial fraud and ineptitude at private testing sites—but would not release those data. It also maintained that the IM-240 testing device government contractors used, mandated by the EPA, which cost $150,000, was superior to other less costly machinery. But again, EPA would not produce any evidence of that, despite our repeated requests.

At one point in this ongoing saga, I hosted a public meeting in Northern Virginia at the request of members of the Virginia General Assembly. Three members in particular, Senator Janet Howell, Senator Jane Woods and Delegate Toddy Puller wanted to hear an EPA official explain the agency's demands first-hand and have the chance to personally question him. Senator Howell, an avowed liberal with whom I had definite differences of political philosophy, seemed to understand exactly what the issues we faced were. She was a great ally in simply demanding straight answers from the EPA about their mandates, their computer modeling, their equipment demand and the impact of their testing program on citizens, particularly working parents and soccer moms who would bear the brunt of long waits at testing garages and the potential ping-pong process.

These three elected officials were a source of encouragement to the DEQ team and to me. When they received the same unsatisfactory answers or non-responses to direct questions, they became allies and were key in crafting the winning plan and legislation to implement it. Each was integral to our success.

To understand how EPA officials could be so indifferent to the actual environment, and so much more concerned with imposing control from Washington, it may help to review the mechanics of how the agency deals with the states. In simple terms, what voters need to understand is that the agency, in its official actions, doesn't focus on air or water quality directly. It issues air-quality credits solely on the basis of how well its edicts are obeyed. If a state is carrying out specific EPA approved tasks, but air quality is getting worse, there is no direct immediate consequence. If a state is improving air quality dramatically, but isn't doing as the EPA commands, it is in trouble for the latter, and receives no reward for the former. As a practical matter, over a period of many years, environmental improvement has some inevitable indirect feedback, of course. But it plays no direct role in the way EPA carries out the laws.

It worked like this: The EPA required states to submit implementation plans describing how they intended to earn the air-quality credits necessary to retain their federal highway funds. But the EPA very narrowly defined what intentions were acceptable and seemed pre-emptively hostile to innovation. For instance, it refused to allow Virginia to earn EPA credits by using remote-sensing—the highly efficient technique where an operator on the side of the road beams an infrared ray into a car's exhaust plume, immediately registering its pollution content. The offending polluter would be sent a notice to have the car inspected, and if confirmed as necessary, be required to undertake repairs that would focus resources public and private on clearing the air.

By contrast, a State *could* earn credits by using EPA schemes to restrict motorboating, lawn mowing, or fireplaces in new homes. (Of course, had the Allen Administration done so, the EPA would have distanced itself from the public outcry, claiming such unpopular bans were the state officials' choice. Contrary to Vice President Gore's later comments about leaders doing and defending the "hard right," EPA always wants someone else to take responsibility for actions it imposes hegemonically.)

If Virginia instituted remote sensing as a core element of its plan in defiance of the EPA, the state would earn no credits even if air quality improved. But as it long as it followed an EPA-approved plan, the state would earn full credit even if air quality deteriorated. Thus states that improved the environment could be penalized, and those that polluted the air could be rewarded because the environment was a secondary issue. What mattered was not substance, but servility.

Learning of the state's plan to object to centralized testing, the EPA informed Allen on June 2 that our state plan—which we hadn't even officially submitted—would be found unacceptable when we did. In a letter that read almost like a ransom note, Kostmayer warned he would hold $400 million in federal highway money unless Virginia did things "our way."

"EPA will consider reinstating [the funds]," Kostmayer wrote, "if Virginia submits new evidence that it is firmly committed to implement an enhanced [centralized testing] program." To me, that was a revealing penalty. "If their goal truly is clean air," I said, "then why would they bar transportation projects, which were started in the first place to alleviate congestion and reduce air pollution from motor vehicles?"

"We needed to get their attention," Kostmayer said, defending the tone of the letter. "The Governor has given every indication that he does not want to do it our way."

Two weeks later I submitted Virginia's plan, which contained something of a new wrinkle in state plans, as far as we could determine. In our plan, we indicated that Virginia was going to achieve a number of improvements in air quality through a novel device: We were going to start requiring that federal agencies and employees obey environmental laws and contribute to environmental improvement. The federal government operated the largest fleet of vehicles in the state. Virginia would require those 5,000 federal fleet automobiles to convert to clean-burning fuels. If the Pentagon were, say, Philip Morris, for example, no one would blink at that. Our plan provided that entities that employing more than 1,000 persons in a single location or close proximity in Northern Virginia (most of which were federal agencies) would have to eliminate free parking as a perquisite. They would need to offer incentives to employees to ride share, offer emissions testing by mobile testing companies in their parking lots to employees participating in car pools, or employ other innovative ideas to reduce their contribution to air pollution.

As novel as these measures might sound, they were arguably within Virginia's rights—and certainly, hard for one federal agency to argue against. Best of all, they fit elegantly within the EPA's credit system. Even if these measures produced little improvement in air quality, they generated credits.

For me personally, it was with some satisfaction that we submitted this plan because it asserted, in relief, an important principle. I believe in fair application of the laws, in which government and its officials are not above the law. It was only fair for the feds to abide by the same standards they impose on the citizenry at large. (With reasonable exceptions: Army tanks may not be able to meet clean air standards, and so on.)

"If the federal government is serious about cleaning up the air in Northern Virginia," I said, "we expect them to comply with this mandate." I wasn't alone in considering turn-about fair play. "If [the EPA's edict] is prohibitive to the federal government," pointed out Virginia Congressman James Moran, "then it certainly is to state and local governments"—the difference being "they have to balance their budgets where, obviously, we don't."

As if my proposal regarding federal employees hadn't rankled the EPA enough by exposing Clinton Administration hypocrisy and lack of sincerity in measurable results, I steadfastly insisted on continuing to test and repair vehicles at private garages. But to ensure that testing would be sufficiently rigorous, I supported the plan developed by DEQ personnel after numerous meetings with the citizens of Northern Virginia and several public hearings. Virginia would continue to improve state training, testing, and certification of emissions inspectors. We would inspect the inspection equipment and mandate upgrades where needed. We would train and test repair technicians, and conduct more frequent random and undercover station inspections. And we would make use of remote-sensing devices to identify cars that appeared to be gross polluters so owners could be notified to have them repaired—and, conversely, to identify automobiles that tested clean so their owners could be relieved of their next scheduled garage test.

In sum, Virginia's plan would impose tougher standards to protect the environment without needlessly inconveniencing drivers.

The EPA said *no.*

Without presenting any supporting data, the agency announced Virginia's plan would not cut air pollution to required levels. It claimed to have determined that by computer analysis, but refused to show me or any of my technical experts the statistical model. Fairfax Supervisor Bob Dix, who was fighting the battle locally, also asked to see scientific data and was provided mere anecdotes.

States that had conceded were beginning to see what a mistake they had made. Though I was told repeatedly Virginia was the only resistant state, that was not true. To be sure, I was a leader in the fray. But centralized emissions testing was proving to be a nightmare in states that had already implemented it, and a dozen other states—fearful they were next in the EPA's sights—were watching Virginia closely. Pennsylvania and Texas, both with Democratic administrations at the time, were among the states watching.

This kind of support cheered me and stiffened my resolve. While attending a multi-state conference, I was approached by an official from Vermont. "I don't agree with you on anything," he told me. "I'm a liberal. But keep fighting for Virginia's right to do things its way." After only one month of centralized emissions testing, Maine's leaders were flooded with complaints of faulty equipment, untrained workers, long lines, inaccurate results, and hundreds of dollars spent by car owners on unnecessary repairs.

New Jersey Senator Bill Bradley wrote a letter to EPA Administrator Carol Browner asking if he and 14 other Congressmen might meet with her to discuss their "serious concern about the implementation of the Clean Air Act Amendments." Bradley reminded Browner that Congress had directed the EPA "to provide the states with continued reasonable flexibility to fashion effective, reasonable, and fair programs"—instructions the agency was defying.

"The state is especially concerned," wrote Bradley, "over EPA's refusal to allow any substitute for its preferred IM-240 tests and its rejection of the benefits of test-and-repair facilities for the majority of motorists."

Meanwhile, after rejecting our plan, the EPA gave us two weeks to come up with a different plan. I requested a meeting. "I need to be able to sit down across the table from you [Kostmayer] and see exactly what you want," I said. Kostmayer had agreed. And so there I sat, on July 29, 1994, listening to him concede the central problem with Virginia's plan was its reliance on private citizens rather than the federal government.

Frustrated but determined to resolve the situation, I presented my next idea: How about state-contracted inspectors leasing bays from private garages so they could set up shop adjacent to repair workers but remain under separate controls? Drivers would not be so inconvenienced, and the EPA's separate-but-equal scheme would be met. Moreover, there would be strict penalties—including loss of operating licenses—if the test and repair stations were found to be colluding.

Kostmayer said the EPA would consider this option. I was optimistic. "It appeared to me that they were disposed to incorporate our plan," I told a reporter after the meeting. "I expect a phone call in the next 24 hours [from EPA saying] that it is a good plan."

The phone didn't ring until 5:45 p.m. the following Wednesday. My Deputy Secretary, Tom Hopkins, took the call. Offering no explanation, an EPA official told him Virginia's second proposal was a no-go as well. Unless an acceptable plan was submitted by Friday, the agency would withhold the state's highway funds.

The next day, August 4, Hopkins and Deputy Transportation Secretary Shirley Ybarra held a conference call with the EPA. Pressed to explain why Virginia's proposal was denied, Thomas Maslaney of EPA's air division held to the party line: There were no data indicating Virginia's plan would work. Candidly, the EPA officials offered a second argument that probably was a more accurate indication of their real thinking: If Virginia succeeded, that could serve to reopen the debate in other states. That excuse resonated with Congressman Moran as well.

"They've been able to intimidate almost every other state," he noted, and would be weakened politically if Virginia prevailed.

EPA officials argued that no combination of technology or security measures could alleviate the conflict-of-interest associated with such programs. Evidence continued to mount that the agency's plan was no better, and arguably inferior, but the EPA was so deeply committed to this will struggle that it seemed to fear any revision in its position. Comparison tests conducted in Georgia between test-only sites and test-and-repair shops found no appreciable difference in the accuracy of diagnoses. Nor was it accurate for the EPA to suggest test-only sites made fewer errors. In New Jersey's, inspectors using the IM-240 equipment failed to recognize non-compliant vehicles 40 percent of the time. In Maryland's, the mistake rate was 69 percent.

But the EPA seemed committed to winning what it perceived as a holy war at any cost. Kostmayer had become convinced Allen and I were sinister. If we opposed EPA's specific plan, we were opposed to environmental protection *per se.*

If that were true, then why had the EPA recommended the year before a plan almost identical to the one it now refused to allow in Virginia? In a March 1993 memo to state governments, Richard Wilson of the EPA suggested four means of testing fleet vehicles for pollution. One called for a state contractor to conduct emissions testing at the garage where the vehicles were maintained—precisely what I had proposed.

Moran obtained a copy of the memo and distributed it August 8th at a press conference held by Virginia's congressional delegation. "EPA allows this for its fleets," Moran said. "Federal vehicles are allowed to do this. Why it's okay for them but not okay for the federal taxpayers is beyond me."

It was gratifying—and reassuring—for me to see the way elected members of both parties supported us and opposed the EPA. If there was any doubt who was behaving in a cooperative way, and who was waging war, it was all but put to rest as Moran and a number of other Democrats rallied to Virginia's defense.

Republican Senator John Warner, who had convened the press conference, called the agency's demands "unreasonable and unrealistic," a characterization that had the implicit bipartisan support of Democratic Congresswoman Leslie Byrne, Republican Congressman Frank Wolf, and Democratic Senator Chuck Robb—all present. Warner threatened to uphold EPA appointments if the agency did not become more reasonable. Byrne blasted the EPA for getting "caught up in a technocratic battle" and said over the weekend she had asked White House Chief of Staff Leon Panetta to investigate the EPA's truculence.

"We're taking this to the highest levels," warned Byrne. "This is not just an EPA problem." Robb nodded.

The next day, under Warner's letterhead, the delegation wrote a letter to Browner, reminding her of the law. "As you will recall," they wrote, "in our letter of June 17, 1994, the Virginia Delegation requested that the agency follow the statute and implementing regulations which provide that 'EPA will consider State Implementation Plans (SIP) submissions designed to demonstrate that decentralized, test-and-repair programs are equally effective to a centralized program.'"

There was broad press support for Governor Allen's position as well. "We need clean air," the *Fairfax Connection* editorialized. "But common sense suggests it can be achieved without the potential monster of centralized testing." Norfolk's *Virginian-Pilot,* a paper normally opposed to our Administration, ridiculed Kostmayer's insistence that a test-only program would not impose any hardship on Virginia. "Easy for Kostmayer to say," scoffed the editors. "He is not likely to have to explain to his boss that he needs to take a day (maybe two) off to have his car tested….This is a federal power grab, pure and simple." *Reason* magazine reported on a pilot program in California. "Dollar for dollar, remote sensing cleaned the air 60 times better than mandatory car-pooling," researchers found—and predicted that, on the basis of just such efficiency, the EPA would disallow the program. "If remote sensing can pinpoint the real culprits at very low cost," they reasoned, "the air-quality justifications for other broad-based command-and-control programs are vitiated...If remote sensing ever catches on, lots and lots of people like Mr. Kostmayer are going to have to get real jobs. The air would be cleaner, it's true, but that's not their concern." The *Arlington Journal* editorialized, "If state officials had any real backbone, they'd tell the Environmental Protection Agency to take its overwrought proposal to test auto emissions and stick it up a tailpipe somewhere." The influential *Richmond Times-Dispatch* added, "The Environmental Protection Agency's threat to shut down road projects in Northern Virginia unless the state submits an acceptable plan for testing car emissions is yet another demonstration that what enviromuddlists want to protect most is their own power."

By refusing to buckle under, Allen and I were creating tremendous problems. Because pseudo-ideology, not science, drove the agency's mandates, its only weapon was intimidation. With Virginia refusing to be intimidated, though, Kostmayer was in a quandary.

Prudently, Kostmayer withdrew his threat of immediate sanctions and declared a cooling-off period until September 21. That bought him time, but earned him the enmity of environmental activists. The Sierra Club and the American Lung Association—both devotees of harsh government regulation—filed suit in U.S. District Court, demanding the EPA punish Virginia. They eagerly insisted the state lose its highway funds until it agreed to the more punitive plan, knowing that relieving congestion is demonstrated to have improved air quality. In particular, they wanted to block the path of Disney's America, a project Allen supported. Sierra Club lawyer Howard Fox accused the feds of backing off in Virginia because of officials' "completely unwarranted" protests.

Moran and Warner wanted Browner to review Virginia's proposal personally. They wanted to hear her offer a credible reason for why the plan warranted rejection. "EPA says the latest plan doesn't fit within their definitions just because they didn't think of it first," Moran theorized.

Despite the partisan divide between him and us, Moran worked tirelessly to protest the attack on the integrity of the service station operators and protect the legitimate interest of his constituents, against bullying from members of his own party. I appreciated his approach at the time, and respected him for his willingness to stand with us. Moran proved, as I believe George Allen did, that clean air and water isn't just a Democratic or Republican concern; it's an American one.

In September, Moran and the other members of our Virginia Congressional delegation scheduled a meeting with Browner, hoping to work out a compromise. At the last minute, Browner inexplicably and abruptly canceled after learning officials from Richmond would be joining their Congressmen. I'm told Browner refused to have the meeting if I or anyone else from the Allen Administration was in the room. That didn't sound to me like she was willing to work with the state.

Ever persistent, Moran tried appealing to Al Gore's interest in reinventing government, writing to the Vice President:

> We share your goals on the need to make government work more efficiently to serve the needs of all Americans. That is why we are particularly concerned that the EPA is pursuing a policy of forcing all states to adopt an unnecessarily inflexible emissions testing program... Congress specifically authorized EPA to allow the states flexibility in creating emissions inspections programs that would reduce emissions but not overburden drivers. However. the system of credit EPA has devised makes it virtually impossible for a state, no matter how workable its program may be, to institute anything but a system that incorporates test-only stations using expensive analytical equipment.
>
> Despite these obvious problems, the EPA remains insistent on the issue. We would be very grateful for anything you could do to bring sensibility to EPA's regulations with regard to emissions testing.

Gore, to our knowledge, did not respond.

All sides were growing weary a few weeks later when Virginia's congressional delegation and I again met with Kostmayer, who now was joined by Mary Nichols, Assistant EPA Administrator for Air. (Nichols was the official who tried to impose the California car on much of the country, though she later did a sensible 180 degree turn and supported our 49-state car proposal, having denounced it as pro-pollution for more than a year.) Virginia offered yet another proposal—a hybrid program like the one the EPA had approved for California. Under the new plan, cars six years old and older would be tested with the more sensitive new equipment; newer cars would be tested with less sophisticated tools. Both tests would be performed at local garages, but by independent contractors, who would lease space at 75 to 100 local garages. The tone of the meeting went well; Virginia's delegation was encouraged. "We got past I guess what I call bureaucratic posturing that sometimes occurs on both sides," said Robb. After the meeting, Nichols and I talked further, and I thought we had reached consensus.

The state's newspapers reported "a tentative agreement" had been reached between Virginia and the EPA. "Governor George Allen and Secretary of Natural Resources Becky Norton Dunlop deserve credit big time for sticking to their guns and making EPA run up the white flag," the *Virginian-Pilot* editorialized in an October 9th piece. "Forcing the EPA to accept a different testing program is indeed a victory...."

The next day from my Richmond office I wrote a thank-you note to Robb and Warner, expressing my appreciation for their help in a battle I believed was now over. "After you left the meeting yesterday," I wrote, "Mary Nichols and I agreed to have our technical people meet on October 20, at which time Virginia will share further details of our plan, which was approved conceptually by...Nichols yesterday." I looked forward to wrapping up the deal at the meeting on October 20.

Instead, the peace treaty came unraveled. Even I became discouraged by the deteriorating tenor of negotiations. EPA staff offered no constructive suggestions, and they steadfastly refused to offer guidance of any sort as to what might make our proposal more acceptable to them. EPA's approach, from my perspective, had been merely to criticize and find flaws in whatever Virginia proposed.

At this point, EPA had tacitly agreed that our approach worked. They had verbally agreed to it, and drafted a plan based on it, even if they ultimately couldn't bring themselves to sign it. After all that had happened, the agency decided it could live with nothing less than Gosplan.

Not long afterwards, Browner came to Richmond to meet her Virginia supporters. A small group gathered at the Chesapeake Bay Foundation's office. There Browner assured them the "other side has the easy rhetoric; we have substance on our side." The fact that even her fellow Democrats in Virginia's congressional delegation opposed the EPA's insistence on centralized emissions testing did not cause her to question for a moment that the plan might be misguided, or to change her us-versus-them mentality. No, to Browner it demonstrated not a difference of opinion but "backsliding on environmental issues."

While she was in Richmond, Browner made no attempt to meet with either me or the governor, which suggested she lacked the customary stature one would expect of a person in her position. Seasoned politicians don't confuse political differences with personal affronts. Even Ronald Reagan and Tip O'Neill were friends after 6 p.m. It also demonstrated the depth of contempt in which Browner held Virginia's officials.

On November 3, Ann Loomis, a senior professional staff member from Senator Warner's office, told my staff she was hearing through the grapevine that the EPA was merely stringing Virginia along and intended to pull the plug after Election Day 1994. Ann was a tremendous asset for Virginia during these discussions providing insight and intelligence from her post on the Hill and her years of experience. Virginia's Washington D.C. liaison staff was in constant contact with Ann during these negotiations. I decided during these days that she would always be on my list of necessary allies in any dealings with the Executive

Branch. Knowledgeable about the environmental statutes, she was also a great tactician and enabled our administration and Senator Warner to work as a strong team for Virginians.

Following up on this message from her about the grapevine, I informed the governor that our prospects were looking bleak. Neither of us ever had been willing to forfeit the state's share of highway funds. As bad as it would be for the EPA to penalize Northern Virginia drivers, it would be even worse for all Virginia drivers to have their fuel tax road money snatched away by the federal government. With state Secretary of Transportation Rob Martinez, the Governor, and I discussed contingencies.

Running out of options, our Administration awaited a November meeting.

Fortunately, that meeting proved unnecessary. Ultimately, what saved Virginia from the Browner Gosplan was the same thing that intervened in a number of other cases: democracy. But a funny thing happened on the way to a quorum: Republicans gained control of Congress. Suddenly the balance of power shifted and the EPA was on the defensive. It was almost pathetic to see arrogant lords reduced to groveling servants.

"Voters have sent a message that they want less confrontation and more cooperation. I think we can do a better job of that," said Kostmayer on November 30, in preliminary remarks before announcing he was offering Virginia…more confrontation and less cooperation. Almost as a last hurrah, the EPA rejected the state's third proposal. Nonetheless, Kostmayer had the air of a zealot going off the cliff with the flag flying. With the GOP now in charge of Congress, he knew the jig was up.

Following a woodshed meeting with the new congressional leadership, Browner, too, was conciliatory. Suddenly she could feel the pain of potentially inconvenienced drivers. Browner said it was fine for states to use less expensive equipment than the IM-240. If remote sensing would reduce pollution, hey, that was okay with her, too. Maybe states would want to concentrate more on power plants or getting older, polluting cars off the road.

"The underlying agenda is quite simply to make sure the Clean Air Act can be implemented in a way that is consumer-friendly, cost-effective, and makes sense." It sounded like me, but the statement was made by Carol Browner, explaining the EPA's grudging reversal.

Some time later, a colleague asked me if it didn't bother me that Browner, after denouncing my position as anti-environmental, had basically adopted it as her own—and was even using my language. I thought about it. "Maybe a little," I smiled. "But you know what? I hope she believes it and keeps on doing it."

It was Senator John Warner and Congressman Tom Bliley though who really brought home the victory for Northern Virginia drivers—and it was with an amendment to the National Highway System Designation Act. To the end, Browner failed to work with Virginia, notwithstanding her new rhetoric. The new Republican majority in the House and Senate did act to provide to the states the flexibility in emissions testing that provided Virginia relief and victory.

Today, more than 350 private auto repair centers and service stations successfully conduct inspections and repairs of autos for the citizens of Northern Virginia in the Aircheck Virginia system launched by the Allen Administration.

4. Reinventing Virginia's EPA

Peter Schmidt's résumé was one of the best things that ever landed on my desk in Richmond. Three months into my service as Secretary of Natural Resources, and in the midst of the crunch of business that descends on a state capital during the winter legislative session, I was looking for the right man to head up our Department of Environmental Quality. Our state's equivalent of the federal Environmental Protection Agency, DEQ was probably the most important of the eight departments under my secretariat. Schmidt not only looked right for the job, but seemed a natural complement to me and others on the A-Team.

I had lived in Northern Virginia for over twenty years, but had little professional experience dealing with Richmond. Peter was a graduate of the University of Virginia in Charlottesville and a resident of the Commonwealth for much of his life. He also had a background in dealing with the issues of waste management from some years as president of Agglite Corporation. Agglite made light-weight concrete from fly ash, a lime and silica compound derived from coal-burning power plant emissions. Not only did the invention turn a handsome profit, it solved a huge waste-disposal problem: Virginia alone produces more than one million tons of fly ash every year. Schmidt brought needed experience from industry to my team, but was not a captive of industry. In fact, he was liked and respected by the environmental regulators who had dealt with him.

Schmidt was well built, with reddish-blond hair and bright blue-green eyes that made you feel he was a straight shooter—which he was. While businesslike and to the point, the ruggedly handsome Schmidt had much hail-fellow-well-met in him. Thoroughly professional, Peter wound up not only winning over regulators in his own department, but establishing a good working relationship with EPA officials in Washington and Philadelphia. Friendly, reasonable, and resourceful, Schmidt was no less tough than the rest of us, but he seemed to put the EPA bureaucrats at their ease.

Schmidt came to my attention late one March Sunday evening as my husband George helped me plow through memos and résumés. Having served as Assistant Secretary of Agriculture in Ronald Reagan's Administration and as chief of staff for a U.S. Senate Committee, my husband understood the workings of government. He knew the sort of employees I would need as Secretary of Natural Resources. Aside from that, he was a devoted husband, which more than anything else explained why he was spending a Sunday night at my office helping me.

I had eight agencies in my secretariat, each requiring specialized attention. Yet, among the eight, the most urgently in need of attention was the Virginia Department of Environmental Quality. The previous year, the legislature had cobbled together the DEQ from the state's former air, water and waste agencies. The addition of just another layer of bureaucracy and lack of a clearly articulated vision meant that the civil servants there spent a good bit of their time and effort on bureaucratic infighting.

The DEQ was the central nervous system of the state's environmental regulations. It issued the state's permits, dealt with complaints from citizens, and monitored water and air quality. The department supervised environmental clean-up projects and reviewed other projects for environmental-law compliance. It had life or death control over virtually every government, business and private activity that involved air emissions, waste-water discharges, or waste disposal. If the DEQ proved ineffectual in working out an effective way to implement the many state and federal environmental laws and regulations, little else I might accomplish for Virginia would matter.

So, I was just delighted when my husband, George said, "Becky, you are not going to believe this!" He had stumbled onto a résumé attached to a letter to Governor Allen that said, "George, if you knew Peter Schmidt, you'd like him a lot. I hope you will consider him for a leadership position in your Administration." As he handed me the letter, I stared at the résumé as if Regis Philbin asked me if this was my final answer to a softball question. I exclaimed to my husband that we could suspend the DEQ search: "I think we've found the one!"

There was one problem: Peter Schmidt had not applied for a job. A friend had recommended him for the Solid Waste Advisory Board or some comparable volunteer position. But judging from his resume, I considered Schmidt impeccably qualified to head the DEQ, and knew that Governor Allen would, too. His career testified to the happy marriage possible between industry and improving the environment. Eager to speak with him, I called Schmidt at home that very evening and asked if he ever had thought about working for state government. Characteristically, his answers were friendly in tone, but to the point. "No, I haven't." Would you consider it? "Well, I'll think about it." The conversation ended with the understanding he would call me no later than Tuesday.

Monday morning Schmidt called and Tuesday he came to my office for a visit. I showed him a draft plan for shifting the DEQ's power from Richmond to regional offices and consolidating the separate air, waste, and water sites into a half-dozen one-stop shops. A career DEQ employee had written the draft, but it reflected my ideas as well as those career civil servants in the department who had given me their ideas for reinventing what was, in a sense, their department.

"Is this concept something you agree with and think you could implement?" I asked. "Would you take this notebook and study what we have put down on paper? Call and let me know if you think it is an idea you think would be good for Virginia and the environment."

Schmidt assured me he would study the paper and call me in a few days. He called to say he thought it was a good idea but would like to work through it with the top people at DEQ if the Governor selected him for the top job. That was good enough for me. "Peter Schmidt?" said George Allen, when I made the recommendation. "I played rugby at UVA with a Peter Schmidt!" From my description, Allen realized we were discussing the same individual. Once again, Schmidt and Allen would be on the same team—this time, in an even more rough and tumble sport.

We were going to need someone with Schmidt's personal and professional qualities and more. For one thing, the outgoing administration and legislature had initiated a reorganization of the whole Department of Environmental Quality, our state's equivalent of the federal Environmental Protection Agency—but had not finished, and in fact only just begun, to actually carry out the reorganization. Our DEQ was thus in a state of semi-disarray, turmoil, and poor employee morale.

And the political activists were already gearing up to oppose any plans of ours out of the basic suspicion that anything the Allen Administration supported must be bad. Whenever any organization is rebuilt, there is conflict and concern. Change of any sort is unsettling. Even in an environment of trust, change at a regulatory agency raises fears on all sides—from businesses concerned that the new regime will be more harsh, and activists worried it will not be harsh enough; from all their friends in the legislature, press, and the community; and from the regulators themselves, who have devoted their career to an agency. Everyone has gotten used to a certain way of doing things.

Privatization of government functions could be a problem in the session, warned activist Georgia Herbert of the Conservation Council of Virginia. "Professionals hired and paid by the builders may not be as devoted to protecting the public health, safety, and welfare as governmental employees," she said. Anne Hayes of Moving People in Northern Virginia said that region needed "enabling legislation to allow them to implement employee trip-reduction ordinances," which is envirospeak for limiting the freedom to drive, á la Al Gore's dread of the automobile. Patti Jackson of the Lower James River Association was worried that lawmakers might again try to require a putting a public price tag on regulation, which could diminish its popularity. "Legislation has been proposed for the past three years to require a cost-benefit analysis prior to the adoption of any state regulation," she warned. "Exhaustive studies would cost the state a lot of money and delay the adoption of regulations unnecessarily."

The professional activists shared a common goal: more government regulation. They also wanted a clean environment, as did all Virginians, but if they could have the latter without the former, would their mission be fulfilled? Were they environmentalists first—or advocates for more government regulations first?

Late in his term, former Governor Doug Wilder pushed through legislation consolidating Virginia's four principal environmental regulatory agencies—the previously separate State Water Control Board, the Department of Waste Management, the Department of Air Pollution Control, and the Council on the Environment—into a new Department of Environmental Quality. The plan was to take effect April 1, 1993, but was in fact barely half begun by the time of the fall election (that November). Little progress had been made toward structuring the new department up to the time when Allen took office in January 1994 except adding layers of managers, new buildings, and a million dollars worth of new furniture.

As the legislative session began in the winter of 1994, opponents of the reorganization in the General Assembly and the business community encouraged me to reverse course. I listened with care and sympathy—certainly the last thing I wanted to do was to be party to making the state's environmental regulatory apparatus more unwieldy than it already was. Yet as sympathetic as I was to their apprehension about bureaucracy, I felt strongly that I needed to think carefully about this new structure. I wanted the Governor to be able to make his own decision about the best course for his Administration in determining exactly how we were to carry out our responsibilities.

It was also apparent from interviews that had taken place during the transition that some among those who opposed the new DEQ had another concern. Developing relationships with individual regulators takes time and effort. Without even necessarily assuming anything improper, a carefully cultivated personal relationship in the individual agencies can help lubricate the permitting process. What Ronald Reagan described as the Iron Triangle was alive and well in Virginia. There was a certain symbiotic relationship between the environmental regulators and the regulated community that suited just fine those "grumpy old men" that had run Virginia politics from their vantage point in the General Assembly for so many, many years.

The "dirty little secret" of environmental regulation worked like this. The legislature would enact bold, but vague statutes. The regulatory boards and agencies would write strict and burdensome regulations, but provide top officials with plenty of flexibility to make exceptions. Those exceptions were always made easier if the entity seeking a permit or facing a sanction were to employ just the right lobbyist to approach just the right Delegate to urge "most earnest consideration" for the exception sought by the lobbyist and its client. The record is replete with exceptions for those entities crafty enough and wealthy enough to retain operatives of the political class to make their case. This little Iron Triangle was about to be disrupted, and the old order didn't like the prospects. I sympathized with the concerns of the regulated community—some legitimate, some not. But I also believed that the organization of DEQ or any other agency should be what works best for all of the people—not the political class in Richmond.

My critics never gave me credit for equal-opportunity jaundice. I was nearly as wary of some of those deemed to be allies as I was enemies. The real enemy was the tendency of Allen's political opponents to make the environment a political football game.

It also never occurred to Democrats that I gave political opponents their due, as I had done implicitly by endorsing the idea of the Democrat-designed DEQ. If streamlining the process was the goal, I reasoned, then the fewer agencies, the better. So what if it had been my predecessor's idea? It had good potential for reform of a rotten system.

The strongest reasons for the reorganization plan my Democratic predecessor had laid out were substantive. Many scientists and conservation professionals who advised me at that time offered sound scientific evidence that the various aspects of the environment are interrelated and should be considered in a holistic manner when considering the possible impacts on the environment. Part of the essence of authentic environmentalism is the realization that things are inter-related.

I decided not to dismantle the newly formed DEQ but to try to make it work for the people, the economy, and the environment.

I wanted the offices consolidated into "one-stop shopping" centers for permit-seekers. Citizens, small businesses, farmers, and corporations should not have to trek back and forth to different locations for meetings with regulators regarding air, waste, and water permits. This was not how matters stood. In Northern Virginia, the air-permit office was in Springfield, the water-permit office in Woodbridge. Permit-seekers in the Tidewater region were bounced between the air division office in Chesapeake to the waste division office in Virginia Beach to the water division warehouse in Norfolk. In government-speak my idea was to make the organization functional—to replace the separate regulatory schemes, offices, personnel and practices for each respective medium, i.e., air, water, and waste, with combined permitting teams. This would enable environmental licenses for activities with an impact on all three media to be issued from one location by a team of permit writers with expertise in air, water, and waste. The purpose of this functional reorganization was to assure that the dual functions of compliance (trying to get polluters to cooperate with us) and enforcement (punishing those who wouldn't) would be made more effective to the benefit of the quality and condition of the environment.

This functional concept was innovative, revolutionary, and, to me, quite logical. It had been discussed in theory for years. But it was not being practiced anywhere, even though many knew instinctively that the hodgepodge media-based systems of environmental regulation in place at EPA and all around the country was dysfunctional.

During my first weeks in office—when each day was consumed almost entirely by needs of the Delegates and Senators in the General Assembly—I had been approached one by one by various members of the staff at DEQ. I also sought out and visited many civil servants whose careers had been devoted to improving environmental quality. Those who approached me said they were frustrated by all of the problems of a dysfunctional agency, and suggested that the Allen Administration consider just such a functional approach to carrying out Virginia's environmental regulatory responsibilities. These officials had listened carefully when I had spoken about the importance of government being a helpful servant rather than a fearsome master.

The functional approach was more than theory, they said. It could work in Virginia, and they hoped the new Administration would give it a chance.

So, I commissioned one of these clear-thinkers to help me draw up just such a plan. I warned him and his allies that my experience in Washington caused me to believe that an effective functional plan would upset the Iron Triangle brigade, and would bring down the ire of EPA on Virginia because it would threaten its own dysfunctional status-quo. There might even be reprisals.

To this day, because of the political environment in Richmond, it is prudent that this public servant's contribution remain anonymous. But he went forward undeterred. It was his draft plan I handed to Peter Schmidt. And when Schmidt was named to head our environmental department by Governor Allen, he set about working with DEQ professionals to finalize a plan along those lines that they could implement.

Peter knew instinctively that if we wanted the new plan to succeed, he must have the support of the best and the brightest. That included career public servants who would be Peter's key lieutenants at DEQ. As he tells it, "...we formed a task group largely of middle managers, but permit writers too, and asked, 'Where do we want to go as an agency? What's the best for DEQ?' And they drove the process and reaffirmed to me what I suspected, that we wanted to be a regional entity." Cross training, streamlining, decentralizing authority, and ensuring that those employees who wanted to pursue a more scientific or technical career path rather than a supervisory one could do so. These were all elements of our new way of doing business.

Schmidt announced in August 1994 the functional reorganization of the DEQ. Its 16 separate offices had been consolidated into six regional offices, reflecting the state's major watersheds. Instead of each region having three directors—separate lines of authority for air, waste, and water—a single regional director would be responsible for all three. In the process, Schmidt eliminated 122 positions: 71 employees took early retirement, 20 were dismissed, and 31 vacant positions were eliminated. The DEQ's streamlined operation was expected to save the taxpayers millions.

Particularly crucial was the relocation of field agents and professional staff out of Richmond into the regions for which they would be responsible. Regional directors were based in the regions they were selected to supervise, which had the dual advantage of making them all more familiar with the territory while giving them a vested interest in the quality of the area's environment in which they and their families would live.

Announcing the new organization, Schmidt explained, "The Allen Administration has shifted the emphasis from the headquarters to the regions, which will result in increased quality and timeliness of permits and help the regulated community continue to improve and enhance the environment." To Brett Burdick of DEQ's response and remediation section, the plan made a lot of sense. "You can tailor your response program to your clientele, so to speak," he said. "For instance, the Roanoke region won't have to be prepared for a shipping channel collision, and the Virginia Beach region won't have to prepare for a coal-mine explosion. Kip Foster of the Roanoke region's water division said, "We've been asking for this for a while." Although the reorganization might seem like a simple construction of regional blocs, the new agency was really best understood as having regional administration of permits, remediation, compliance and enforcement in combination with a central support function in Richmond.

That support function was especially important in dealing with outside agencies like the federal EPA. Whatever our authority was in theory—and as a state agency it was supposed to be great—I was finding that many of our policies had to survive a strong challenge from Washington. It was therefore vital to have a team of experts, each at the top of his field, who could deal on a par with the air, water, and solid waste experts, respectively, at the Environmental Protection Agency and with DEQ counterparts in other states. These we had in such career civil servants as Larry Lawson (for water issues), Hassan Vakali (waste), and above all John Daniel (air). A highly capable scientist and career civil servant respected by his peers, Daniel had a personality that, like Schmidt's, enabled him to work effectively with people at the EPA—even when those officials were furious at our Administration and me.

Complete reorganization would take nearly a year, primarily because of office lease constraints, but the more extreme activists quickly declared the not-yet-implemented plan a disaster. Regional offices would be overburdened and unable to perform their tasks, Patti Jackson said. Besides, Virginia already was issuing permits with unseemly haste, she thought. A report showing our state issued environmental permits faster and for less cost than five other Southern states should have been a point of pride. Instead, for our opponents, it corroborated their claim of recklessness at the top. Jackson had expressed to Schmidt early on her concerns about speedy permit issuance, and he had assured her that efficiency wasn't being improved at the expense of enforcement rigor. Indeed, the inherent efficiency of the functional approach increased our effectiveness in going after bad actors who violated the law and their permits, Schmidt assured her. "If the permit [contains] no or few limits," she had grumbled, "then there's nothing to enforce."

I think that the strategy of many professional activists and what they have always understood as their role is to stand in the way of the use of natural resources. Some activists define their environmentalism as opposition to development of any kind (except that undertaken by themselves and their allies, of course). For others, I think, there was simply such a great fear and suspicion of anything that we did, that whatever was good for the economy had to be hurting the environment. The media-specific approach they were used to had created innumerable opportunities for delay, delay, delay. If any of three different offices objected to a particular permit, a project might be derailed. In short, those who view economic progress as a threat to the environment like having as many shots as they could get at the beast.

Now, with a regional official who could make decisions one way or another, projects would be blocked only on the merits as seen by our regional offices. Sheer logistical delay, while companies moved back and forth between multiple offices any one of which could block development, was reduced. Some of the activists wanted no part of permit efficiency—even if it meant improved compliance, remediation, and enforcement. Or, to be more precise, they were convinced the remediation and enforcement would never come—because they were convinced we were devils.

At least on an administrative level, our plan was getting results. The agency was getting its job done and spending less money than originally budgeted. To those who measure good government by its success in wringing money from taxpayers, our administration's mindset was unfathomable and creepy; our success, failure.

Moreover, even without a command-and-control approach, and in the face of expanding economic activity, Virginia's environment was not getting worse, as some had predicted. In fact, there were highly tentative indications it was improving. Naturally, the evidence was far too early for us to make much ado about it at the time—that is one of the difficulties for any environmental administrator. But the measurements that could be taken in the short term were pointing in the right direction. In 1995, Northern Virginia ozone exceeded permissible levels on just 9 days—a dramatic decline from the 72 days of excessive ozone in 1988. Fish and bird populations, some of which were estimated annually, seemed to be improving.

In May of 1996, Schmidt said, essentially, "My work here is done." In two short, but fast-paced years he had put in place a remarkable change at DEQ. He had implemented innovative and valuable changes in structure, culture and results and he wanted to go home to Virginia Beach, to his young family and to private business. He had accomplished a remarkable job. Virginia is greatly indebted to this fine citizen who demonstrated in a very measurable way that a growing economy and an improving environment go hand in hand. When he left in June of 1996, Governor Allen appointed the Deputy Secretary, Tom Hopkins, to replace him.

Hopkins came in amidst a highly politicized election environment—over the next 18 months, there would be a U.S. national election in 1996, and Virginia state elections in 1997. A gentle man averse to conflict, Tom was coming into a free fire zone. Allen's partisan opponents wanted to attack our environmental record, and as the good evidence from air and water was not a promising area for them to exploit, picking apart our organization plan in the press and through quasi-legislative investigations was all that was left to them. In retrospect, it was unfortunate that we selected this mild-mannered attorney, who though a highly effective Deputy Secretary, had not needed to command and defend his own ship. It was also a measure of our opponents, however, that they would adopt a seek-and-destroy attitude towards one of the gentlest and most sincere persons I've ever met.

EPA's Region III also had a new administrator, W. Michael McCabe. McCabe's style was not that of an attack dog, but at age 43 he had a seasoned past as an earnest environmental activist. At the time of his appointment as the Clinton-Gore head of EPA's regional office in Philadelphia, he had spent eight years as a political operative for Senator Joseph Biden, Democrat from Delaware. In 1979 and 1980 he was the chief organizer for Earth Day '80 and was coordinator of environmentalists for Jimmy Carter, organizing environmental activists in 10 states for the Carter-Mondale ticket. He began his government career as a legislative assistant for Senator Gary Hart, and his newest political appointment at EPA came just in time for an election-year assault against Virginia's Republican Administration. McCabe had taken over after Peter Kostmayer left the post.

McCabe now had a real environmental problem on his hands. Tap-water in Washington, D.C., was contaminated—again. The level of coliform bacteria found in City water samples exceeded federal standards. City officials increased substantially the amount of chlorine added to the water and advised some residents to boil first what they planned to drink. Carol Browner even stepped in, announcing that the EPA would begin independent testing of the city's supply of drinking water. The District's continued violation of federal water-quality she said, reflects "a continued pattern of deterioration, neglect, and uneven operation." EPA had been negotiating a consent order for nearly a year.

Many people considered it incredible that the capital city of the world's greatest nation lacked life's most essential element, clean drinking water, but McCabe apparently had bigger fish to fry. How could he be expected to ensure safe drinking water for Washington when he had to contend with Virginia, where the environment was improving under the stewardship of people who spurned his and Carol Browner's micromanagement? Instead of the District, McCabe seemed to consider Virginia his most important enforcement target.

As the 1996 election campaign season came into full swing, McCabe suddenly became upset because the Allen Administration wasn't imposing fines and penalties on businesses sufficiently to suit him. In September, he wrote Hopkins complaining that water pollution fines had dropped, as had the number of cases in which fines were sought. Such falling enforcement statistics, said McCabe, "are a signal to the regulated community that Virginia may not be willing to enforce the laws." If that was true, the regulated community was not getting the message. Discharges of regulated pollutants by factories had fallen from 85.2 million pounds for 1993 to 72 million pounds for 1994. "We have a successful record on enforcement because we stress compliance," said DEQ Deputy Director March Bell. "We see enforcement as a tool to improve the environment, not to put a trophy on the wall."

While McCabe kept Hopkins and the new DEQ under attack with one hand, our partisan opponents in the legislature opened their own assault. During the first weekend in October 1996, the Virginia House of Delegates Committee on Conservation and Natural Resources took a retreat to Front Royal, Virginia. I was invited to make a presentation on the status of my various agencies and to discuss some of the key issues we faced as well as to respond to any legitimate concerns of the members of that General Assembly committee.

Of course, we always faced the normal "gotcha" questions from the extremely political and liberal delegate Kenneth Plum, who subsequently became Virginia Democratic Party Chairman. I asked all of my agency chiefs to attend this meeting as I was

70

committed to including my team by allowing them to hear my representation of their work and have them available to provide the details that might be desired since we worked together on the issues and policies. DEQ enforcement director Harry Kelso was also along to summarize the department's progress in the decentralization of the enforcement program.

What the Allen Administration had found after taking over in 1994, Kelso said, was "the four former agency cultures operating under one house, but with a continuation of their respective and very differing cultures and operating rules; multiple offices, formerly operated by the former agencies, not connected within DEQ; and, with respect to enforcement, three different operating schemes.... After considerable examination by the management team, in 1995, DEQ was reorganized to set the agency on a firm directional footing and to set up one agency culture. This new culture was designed to build on the institutional expertise of the former agencies, but to operate on the philosophy of today's more modern environmental paradigm and Virginia's new enforcement policy: Compliance first, enforcement second."

The most important vehicle for the Allen opponents in Richmond was the Joint Legislative Audit and Review Commission, or JLARC. This was the highly partisan investigative arm of Virginia's General Assembly, controlled and directed at the time by Democrats. On January 15, 1997, the commission issued a report, the various elements of which had been selectively released and leaked throughout the 1996 political season. Now, with the 1996 elections behind them, it was time for the partisan operatives at JLARC to begin their political machinations to influence the upcoming November 1997 Virginia elections. The JLARC report was a kind of catchall basket for complaints by activists and even Richmond lobbyists, the complaints clustered together as if they were an objective review of Schmidt's reorganization, and Hopkins's management of it.

The report chastised the department for not having a good relationship with the EPA, implying state officials were the aggressors. In fact, Hopkins had been told by the water enforcement staff at EPA's regional offices in Philadelphia that the actions taken against Virginia were ordered by McCabe for political reasons and that the EPA's own enforcement staff had objected to McCabe's behavior. And in most of our disputes with the federal government, leading Democrats such as Virginia Senator Chuck Robb and Congressman Jim Moran backed our position, not the Clinton-Gore Administration.

JLARC also discovered a "weakness" in the water enforcement program, saying DEQ had showed a "reluctance to take strong enforcement action against localities." But as Hopkins pointed out, "It has *always* been the Commonwealth's policy not to impose significant fines against local governments, except in extraordinary cases. Local government budgets do not include appropriations for penalties, and imposing large fines would disrupt their budgetary process. In addition, fining localities will transfer to Richmond dollars that localities typically use to fix the problem causing the violation....This policy exists in most states and is endorsed by EPA through its guidance to states under the Clean Water Act."

I joined Hopkins in defending his department. After reading the draft report, I pointed out to JLARC Director Philip Leone some fundamental points of disagreement. As to the commission's complaint that the agency's decentralization had made it inconvenient for the commission to retrieve files not located in Richmond, I agreed. "Running a distributed field staff certainly presents management challenges," I told Leone, "but it also makes for a more effective strategy" to improve the environment. I was not surprised that commissioners found some workers unhappy with the size of their budgets. All government officials complain that budget constraints limit their ability to do more. Indeed, I pointed out to the commission, "If you interviewed families in Virginia, I expect you would also be told by each that they could do better with more money."

Hopkins and I were not the only ones who found the commission report misguided. "If the purpose" of DEQ "were to collect fines and file suits," said the *Richmond Times-Dispatch,* "then perhaps JLARC would have a stronger case. But DEQ's purpose is to husband the environment—and the fact is that under George Allen's stewardship, the environment is improving. Rather than merely punishing offenders, the Allen Administration has taken a more constructive approach: It seeks to help them clean up their operations, so as to avoid polluting in the future....But this does not satisfy liberals, who cannot congratulate themselves for being the moral superiors of others if they work cooperatively with them."

The commission did not publicize the substantive parts of its findings, such as its conclusions that the department was doing a good job of enforcing air and waste pollution laws and that air quality in the state was improving. Likewise, the report criticized the method by which water quality was monitored, but could not condemn water quality itself, conceding indicators were "mixed." It cited a 1996 report by the DEQ showing that 5 percent of monitored waters were "polluted," up from 3 percent in 1994. But the reason for that was that DEQ had added more monitoring sites, so that regulated pollutants that previously had been dissipated before reaching a monitoring point downstream were now being detected closer to the source. These additional monitoring sites were something that I was enthusiastic about even though I knew the potential for the outcome that did in fact occur. It had long been my conviction that it is the proper role of government to gather better data and employ improved scientific techniques to help identify the true state of the environment. JLARC also had to grudgingly admit that the majority of localities and businesses were pleased with their service from the DEQ and that employee morale was improving.

How did the professional activists take the news? "This just confirmed our worst fears," said Jackson. "There doesn't seem to be a commitment to protecting state waters, which is disturbing."

"I think people should be irate, embarrassed, and woken up," said Sierra Club lobbyist and later Democratic Delegate, Albert Pollard. "This is just an enormous problem."

JLARC had accomplished the purpose for which it then existed, to serve as a political arm of the grumpy old men in the General Assembly who hated the idea of George Allen as Governor and Becky Norton Dunlop as Natural Resources Secretary. We took it all in stride because we knew the commission to be just so much political theater, and we knew we could hold our own and give as well as we got in their contemptible little sideshow.

Interestingly, not a single Delegate sponsored legislation to impose fines and penalties on polluting municipalities.

Though Hopkins began running the DEQ in June of 1996, he could not be confirmed until the legislature reconvened the following winter. So in early February 1997, Hopkins appeared before the General Assembly, where he was met with unprecedented hostility. Enemies of the Allen Administration described Hopkins as "clueless" and "corrupt," insults that were clearly gratuitous because only one lawmaker—William and Mary Professor and Democratic Delegate George Grayson—voted not to confirm him. Surely if they really believed Hopkins to be clueless or corrupt, lawmakers would have withheld their seals of approval.

There were two factors at work. First, on the national level, Bill Clinton was now safely ensconced for a second term. The EPA had no more need to feign cooperation with states, and, in fact, was eager to re-assert its authority, and make an example of states such as Virginia. Within a month of Clinton's second inauguration, Deputy Administrator Fred Hansen killed the EPA's election-year promise to expedite innovative plans developed by states, which it called the "natural laboratory for testing new ideas." A coalition of state officials wrote the EPA complaining, "You appear to be focused on creating great barriers to true innovation. We believe it is a gross error to require all innovative proposals to achieve the superior environmental performance threshold." Their complaints were duly ignored.

In March 1997, ironically, the EPA began reorganizing to comply with Al Gore's reinventing-government directives. Several new offices were established in the agency, which necessitated upheaval. "While we are aware that any restructuring may bring uncertainty," Browner told employees, "we are committed to consulting closely with you and our union partners in carrying out these changes, so as to minimize any disruptions."

Virginia's still Democratically controlled General Assembly, meanwhile, took up the torch in Richmond, forming a kind of second front for EPA's continuing assault on Virginia. In the 1997 session, the legislature ordered Virginia's DEQ to reorganize as well. The Democrats eliminated six positions in the DEQ by statute, simply because they believed—erroneously—that the positions were filled by Allen political appointees. Having complained vociferously during the 1996 election season that the DEQ was not enforcing laws sufficiently, one of the positions they eliminated in 1997 was the department's director of enforcement.

The new organization placed the central office structure into the same functional structure as the six regional offices and re-distributed the workload of the six people that the General Assembly eliminated. In the final shakeout, 29 positions and jobs were eliminated and 34 created. The 29 employees whose positions were "eliminated" were exactly the ones expected to apply for one of the new 34 positions in the agency.

"This is outlandish!" screeched Delegate Ken Plum, one of the grumpiest of the grumpy old men. "This goes way beyond anything the legislature asked for...Be assured we will be looking at this one."

"It is clear that it not only did not implement [our] recommendations," said state Senator Joe Gartlan, more of a gentleman than Plum, but no less grumpy. "It is also clear that this action taken by Mr. Hopkins went way beyond what the commission recommended." State Senator Emily Couric and Delegate Mitchell Van Yahres wrote a letter of protest to the Governor. "This reorganization plan lacks consideration of its effect on many localities and will result in serious damage to the Commonwealth's air and water quality," they presumed to inform him.

EPA opened fire on its front, threatening to withhold more than $1 million in grant money to protest this final change in the agency structure, though it had no evidence that the environment was in any way threatened by the changes. Needless to say, this generated enormous press coverage and kept the "environmental issues" on the front burner of Virginia politics throughout all of 1997.

A fine man and a gentleman, Tom Hopkins was not ready for the kind of unremitting assault that was underway. A few days after the EPA announcement he stood before the panel of legislators who had summoned him for a noon meeting and looked at his watch.

"I figured the reason you all scheduled me for this hour was because you were going to have me for lunch," he said. He didn't realize how right he was. The lawmakers wanted to chew up Hopkins for organizing his agency in the manner he thought necessary to carry out the statutory obligations.

Hopkins explained that, in restructuring the DEQ, he had acted on the advice of the state's Department of Personnel and Training, which told him to lay off and rehire rather than transfer employees because the new positions weren't the same as the old ones. "I would prefer not to have to go this [route] and just move" workers around, Hopkins said. But had he done that, he would have been accused of pre-selecting employees. "It's a no-win situation" he advised the lawmakers.

Delegate Tayloe Murphy was particularly upset about incurring the wrath of the fearsome feds. What if the EPA holds up grants or takes over the DEQ in disapproval? "If that happens," he told Hopkins, "you have done a great disservice not only to the [business] community, but to the environmental community." Plum accused Hopkins of personal "incompetence, inefficiency, and seemingly downright deception."

A quiet, unassuming man, Hopkins had never served in government before I recommended him to be Deputy Secretary. Until then, he had practiced environmental law in Roanoke and worked as an adjunct professor at a local college. When Allen was elected, Hopkins sent his résumé to Richmond, hoping for a supporting role in an administration he supported. *What had he done to warrant such personal attacks for political differences?*

"I am not doing this for political reasons," Hopkins finally said in defense. "I am not a political hack, and I do not appreciate the implication that I am."

McCabe fired off his next salvo a few weeks later:

> The purpose of this letter is to request specific information about the restructuring of the Virginia Department of Environmental Quality (VADEQ), which the Department announced on June 2, 1997. As you know from recent discussions and correspondence, the Environmental Protection Agency is concerned about the effect which the potential loss or transfer of experienced employees and the new structure may have on [your] ability to implement and enforce the federal environmental laws which it has received authority to implement. These concerns were underscored by correspondence and reports I have received from the Virginia Joint Legislative Audit and Review Commission...

McCabe's letter included 16 instructions designed to pile more paperwork on the already overwhelmed Tom Hopkins. Why was a report written for state lawmakers, ostensibly on how better to advise a state agency, passed on to a federal bureaucrat? Could there be any explanation other than McCabe was a political ally who could help harass a mutual enemy? And why did McCabe send copies of the letter to such professional activist groups as the Chesapeake Bay Foundation, Friends of the Rivers of Virginia, the James River Association, the Sierra Club, the Southern Environment Law Center, unless he was trying to score points with them?

Area newspapers agreed that the effort amounted to political harassment. "Don't put it past the EPA to lean on a state close to D.C. for political and media advantage," *The Alexandria Journal* wrote. "In Maryland—which happens to have a Democratic governor—pollution citations, financial penalties, and criminal prosecutions have fallen sharply without any threats from EPA," noticed *The Washington Times*. "Clearly, this is mere political gamesmanship. If the EPA could point to *any instance* where Virginia's environment is deteriorating, then it certainly wouldn't be wasting its time carping about the DEQ's reorganization," *The Richmond Times-Dispatch* nodded.

At the very time this campaign was underway, some notable things happened of a substantive nature involving the environment. The EPA quietly dropped the Hampton Roads area and Richmond from its list of smoggy cities. Having improved steadily for the past four years, Richmond's air quality reached attainment of federal standards as did air quality in Hampton Roads and White Top Mountain, way down in Southwest Virginia. There was progress before George Allen came to office, to be sure. The progress, however, continued and arguably accelerated during the years Allen was in office given the economic development that occurred during his tenure. It certainly did not reverse course, which was what our critics had repeatedly predicted would result from our policies. It was during those years that Delegate George Grayson tried to abolish the Natural Resources Secretariat, saying about me, "No one since General Ulysses S. Grant has posed a greater threat to our resources and our people."

When the DEQ was formed in 1993, my predecessor Elizabeth Haskell said, "The creation of DEQ has given state government a dramatic opportunity to deliver streamlined and more responsive environmental services to the public, not through increased regulation and spending, but through innovative planning, public involvement, and redirected resources. The expected performance of DEQ will be enhanced environmental protection and a strengthened economy, two compatible and critical state goals."

George Allen and I fulfilled that worthwhile endeavor almost word-for-word. In so doing, I made friends of those who cherish the environment, but not those who cherish environmental activism as a means to exercise political control over people's lives. The professional activists had to choose between process and product. Process mattered most.

The painful fact for the activists is that in the absence of a command-and-control approach, and in the face of expanding economic activity, Virginia's environment was not getting worse, as some had predicted. It was improving. This was quite the opposite of what such Delegates Grayson and Plum had predicted for our watch. Naturally, the evidence in 1997 was far too preliminary for us to make much of it at the time—that is one of the difficulties for any environmental administrator. But the measurements that could be taken in the short term were pointing in the right direction. Ozone exceedences dropped significantly over four years. By 1996, 95 percent of Virginia's streams and rivers tested met the federal EPA's "fishable and swimmable" standards for cleanliness, compared to the 60 percent more typical for other states. The once-endangered striped bass population was pronounced completely recovered. Scores of bald eagles, once an endangered species, were now roosting along not just the James River, but the Rappahannock, York, Potomac and other Virginia rivers. Other species such as bear, deer and wild turkey were growing in abundance throughout the Commonwealth. The Chesapeake Bay continued to show measurable improvement, per the objectives established in the 1983 agreement between the states in the Chesapeake watershed. Amounts of regulated chemicals released by Virginia industries continued to show steady reduction. Tire pile and underground storage tank problems that plagued other states and were approaching crisis proportions when we took office were dealt with systematically and became only passing concerns.

As DEQ policy director Mike McKenna said in January, 1997, "Every indicator—every single indicator in air quality and water—shows that air quality and water quality are improving. No data can get around that."

On June 6, 1997 the DEQ's new Northern Virginia Office opened. I spoke at the opening ceremonies before the Open House and tour of the building commenced. "When DEQ was formed in April, 1993, there were 23 waste, water, and air offices scattered throughout the Commonwealth," I said. "Now the three media are under one roof in each of the six regions, and the majority of DEQ professionals are living and working in the communities they serve. The result is better customer service, better problem-solving, and better compliance with regulations intended to benefit the environment....You are at the forefront of the new environmental paradigm that is sweeping the nation."

I believed that when I said it, and believe it more strongly now.

One of the people who helped author that success was not, unfortunately, here to witness the full fruits of his efforts: Tom Hopkins.

Consumed by a political viciousness he did not engage in nor understand, Tom turned inwards, following a path that dissipated his health and well-being. Tom passed away in the spring of 1998 plagued by worry and distraught over the attacks that had been perpetrated upon his integrity and character.

"They killed him," Peter Schmidt told me recently. "They hounded that man to his death." Of course, I knew Schmidt didn't mean it literally, but there is an element of sad truth in what he said.

Tom Hopkins was a fine man. Compared to his tormenters—well, to paraphrase Nick Carroway, he was "better than the whole lot of them."

5. Smithfield

As the May 22, 1996, Water Control Board meeting drew to a conclusion, members were taken aback. Everyone had been prepared for the discussion of "toxic" discharges from Newport News Shipbuilding and assessing the revised regulations for dioxin and heavy metals. But the terms of Smithfield Foods 1991 consent order? That topic was not even on the agenda. The agreement was old news and there were no decisions to make. Why was the company's lawyer, Jim Ryan, now asking for an eleventh-hour reprieve?

Norfolk-based Smithfield Foods operated two meatpacking plants which discharged treated slaughterhouse wastewater into the Pagan River. The company struggled to meet state environmental standards but often failed. Even building its own wastewater treatment plant was not successful. Since 1977, the Commonwealth had taken Smithfield to court twice, threatened to sue four other times, and issued eight consent orders trying to bring the company into compliance with water quality standards.

Phosphorous content was a persistent problem because a certain quantity was inevitable in meat processing. By 1988, the state's restrictions had reached a level impossible for Smithfield— and many other companies—to meet because the standards were based on an analysis of reductions achievable for sanitary human wastes, not industrial wastewater from meat packing operations.

Even environmental activists were sympathetic to the company's predicament. David Bailey, director of Virginia's Environmental Defense Fund, said, "It takes time to work all this out. In a lot of environmental problems, which are getting more and more complex, we can't just set a number and demand compliance....Had the Board had more resources and more time, they might have taken a closer look at categories of discharge they had to deal with, and they might have modified the number a bit."

Smithfield said it had no other choice but to move operations to North Carolina, where restrictions were looser. Faced with the potential loss of a major employer and taxpayer, Virginia regulators fashioned a compromise. In a consent order approved by the Water Board on March 25, 1991, Smithfield agreed to build 17 miles of pipelines from its two plants on the Pagan River to a newly constructed Hampton Roads' Sanitation district treatment plant in Suffolk. Within 90 days of the treatment plant and pipeline's completion, Smithfield would begin pumping its wastewater there. The second plant would hook up within a year. Construction would take four or five years, but after its completion, the plant would stop discharges into the Pagan River altogether. In exchange for Smithfield's willingness to solve the problem permanently, the state committed itself not to penalize the company for its inability to meet the stricter phosphorous limits in the meantime.

The deal was struck during the tenure of a Democratic Governor, Doug Wilder, by a Water Control Board whose members had been appointed by three Democratic Governors—Wilder, Gerald Baliles, and Chuck Robb. There is no evidence that either Democratic Lieutenant Governor Don Beyer, or Democratic Attorney General Mary Sue Terry, objected to the consent order in 1991—nor did the EPA. In fact, the federal agency specifically indicated it had no objections to the arrangement worked out by the state.

Now, five years later, the project was nearly complete. But Smithfield's lawyer was asking for more time. Ryan argued that because the necessary upgrades to the new Suffolk plant were not fully complete, implementation of the deal should be delayed another 18 months. That would spare additional pollution of the James River, into which the effluent would be re-routed, while—coincidentally—saving his client about $3 million in monthly sewage bills.

The state Water Board officials were puzzled. Four members of the board were Allen appointees; they had not been party to the consent order. But they knew the plan had been progressing for years. Was a last-minute delay really necessary? Bert Parolari of the DEQ's Virginia Beach office refuted Ryan's claim, telling the board that the DEQ technical assessment was that the planned sewage shift instead would result in "considerable environmental benefit." Though it was true the improvements being made to the Suffolk plant were not complete yet, chemical screening there was superior to the technology used by Smithfield. "We recommend the earliest possible connection," DEQ's Parolari told the Board. The general manager of Hampton Roads Sanitation District sent word that the Suffolk plant was ready to begin accepting Smithfield's waste and that it was environmentally prudent to do so.

Ryan was not giving up. He said he would at least like the chance to negotiate further with state officials. The board granted his request and agreed to meet with Smithfield the following week.

When word of the board's attempt at congeniality filtered back to me, I called in Tom Hopkins, my Deputy Secretary, and said, "Tom, we can't have this. Our people [on the board] don't know the facts about Smithfield—that it's been an ongoing problem. Didn't the Board's counsel from the Attorney General's office speak up and explain all the legal background on this case, starting with the legal threats back and forth in the mid-80's? Call the Board back in for another board meeting as soon as one can legally be scheduled and urge them not to change the consent order. Tell them Smithfield should just meet the requirements of the [1991] consent order and get this first connection to HRSD (the Hampton Roads Sanitation District) completed on time."

On June 11, 1996, the state Water Control Board met again and unanimously instructed the company to begin piping its wastewater to Suffolk by June 25. "It's time for those folks down there to do what's right and hook up to that line," said Hopkins who had assumed the post of Director of DEQ following Peter Schmidt's return to the private sector. Hopkins added that Virginia was prepared to go to court if Smithfield did not comply. Ryan said his company would make the switch within the next few weeks. The *Virginian-Pilot* reported that "after 19 years of fighting and cajoling the $3 billion company, an end to one of Virginia's worst water-pollution problems appears at hand."

That was only partly true. One of the reasons I had been so adamant about holding Smithfield to the consent order was because DEQ was preparing a civil case against the company to seek penalties for water-quality violations not covered under the consent order. During routine DEQ inspections of Smithfield, the state's environmental officers found consistently excessive amounts of residual chlorine, ammonia nitrogen, and other regulated pollutants being discharged. They also uncovered what the DEQ believed was criminal activity on the part of Smithfield's wastewater treatment manager, Terry Rettig, whom the company fired after finding inconsistencies in wastewater discharge records. The DEQ provided the evidence it had collected to the Commonwealth's Attorney, who pursued criminal matters in the environmental area in the Commonwealth. This Commonwealth's Attorney decided to turn this case over to the U.S. Department of Justice.

Department of Justice attorneys working on this criminal investigation called DEQ criminal investigator Ralph Mayer to make a formal request of DEQ enforcement chief Harry Kelso.

"Would Virginia hold off on taking civil action against Smithfield while the criminal case was being pursued?" the feds asked. They were pursuing Rettig for federal criminal prosecution pursuant to the evidence DEQ has provided, and the state's civil prosecution would interfere with their case. Honoring long-standing policies on conflicting criminal and civil cases, or "parallel proceedings," Kelso agreed.

On July 2, 1996 EPA officials and DEQ staff held a routine meeting in Washington. While I did not attend these meetings, it was reported to me that Amy Clarke of the DEQ gave an account of the Smithfield situation, informing the EPA's Carol Amend that the company had completed connection to Hampton Roads' sewer system, fulfilling part one of its consent order. It was also reported that Smithfield and Hampton Roads Sanitation district were on schedule for the second hook-up scheduled to occur in the spring of 1997. Amend said nothing, which was remarkable because the EPA was preparing its own case against Smithfield, which it referred to the Department of Justice on July 25. Without informing Virginia's DEQ. This was in violation of a 1976 agreement by which EPA delegated the clean water permit program to Virginia. Virginia was told nothing about the action until our regular meeting with the EPA in August when federal investigators asked for the state's input. Hopkins wanted to know why Amend had remained silent when the subject of Smithfield was discussed, indeed, why the EPA had actively concealed its plan of action. EPA refused to explain.

So on August 30, Attorney General James Gilmore, on behalf of the Commonwealth of Virginia proceeded with the civil suit against Smithfield, seeking $3 million for pollution violations not covered under the consent order. The state had legal primacy, after all, as Hopkins reminded McCabe.

The EPA was furious because it knew the state's action likely would block its own enforcement, so the agency enlisted its allies to malign the Allen administration's motives. "Just like the fecal coliform that Smithfield is dumping, this doesn't smell good and someone should come clean," said the Sierra Club's Albert Pollard, who subsequently emerged as a Democratic candidate. Kay Slaughter of the Southern Environmental Law Center said, "I would hope this is not a political pre-emption." Kay had earned her political stripes as a Democratic candidate for Congress against none other than George Allen. I could only imagine what their rhetoric would have been had we not filed suit against Smithfield. Critics, who claimed the governor was coddling a friend, produced campaign finance records showing Smithfield chairman Joseph Luter had contributed $125,000 to Allen's political action committee. More fair-minded observers wondered how the Allen Administration was going to treat its enemies.

The claim that Virginia had hastily cobbled together a lawsuit within days to protect a political ally from federal prosecution was patently absurd to anyone with a rudimentary understanding of law. No rational person believed a lawsuit requiring years of investigation could be prepared in less than a week. Once informed that the federal criminal prosecutors had lifted the stay on civil enforcement, the state resumed working on its civil enforcement case against Smithfield. The state had proceeded when it did, explained DEQ Deputy Director March Bell, because Virginia had been working on its case for months and was ready to go. Waiting for federal prosecutors to complete their own investigation of Smithfield "might take months, if not years," Bell said. Moreover, enforcing the state water laws was the state's responsibility—not the federal government's. "We've been working this case all summer, and then at the last minute, out of nowhere, we learned they were preparing a case and never coordinated with us," explained Bell. "We have primary responsibility for these cases."

The EPA was livid. In a September 19, 1996 letter to Hopkins, McCabe accused the state of being soft on polluters and trying to protect them from federal prosecution. "Enforcement in Virginia has dropped off the charts," McCabe railed, impervious to the explanation that lower enforcement numbers reflected increased compliance with the law. The Governor's spokesman, Ken Stroupe, pointed out the irony of McCabe's hostility.

"The EPA is angry at us because we sued a company for polluting. That seems to be one of the most hypocritical... statements that I have ever seen out of [the Clinton] administration. Imagine that: a state being able to enforce its own laws without the federal government acting as lord and master."

The governor laughed it off. "It's, on the one hand, aggravating for them to be making such charges," Allen said. "On the other hand, it's almost hilarious. Because if I did not say, 'Go ahead and sue 'em,' then they'd be complaining....But, you know, it's an election year."

I, too, was philosophical, understanding the motivation. "Two months before the election, they come out with this malarkey? I think if you check Mike McCabe's history, you'll find out that he is a far-left-leaning Democrat activist. We expect all this will settle down again once the election's over."

If one looks objectively at the timing, it becomes clear that Virginia acted, if anything, with greater alacrity. We filed our civil case only a couple of months after Smithfield's attempt to win a last-minute reprieve from the consent order—and part of that delay reflected our good-faith effort to consult EPA. The federal government's criminal case against Rettig was based on actions he took prior to his firing. Two years later, having taken no action, and having informed us of no case in the making, the federal government decided it wanted to pursue a criminal case—in 1996. Then, after asking Virginia to delay its civil case to assist DOJ's criminal prosecution, the federal government announces—just months before a presidential election—it will file a civil case of its own against Smithfield. It seemed to me that the only suspicious timing was coming not from Richmond, but from Washington.

On October 22, Rettig pled guilty to federal charges that he released illegal amounts of fecal coliform from pig droppings into the Pagan River. That same day, the Justice Department commanded Smithfield to pay $12.5 million in fines or face paying 10 times that much in a federal lawsuit. Twelve days later, shifting from the bad cop role to the good cop, the Justice Department lowered its demand to $3.5 million. If Smithfield wrote a nice check to the feds, everyone could remain friends.

Smithfield chairman Joseph Luter said the company would not pay "one penny" of the fines sought by the EPA. "This is extortion," said Luter. "It's blackmail. It's political. And there comes a time when you have to stand up."

So on December 16, the federal government sued Smithfield for nearly $125 million over some 5,000 water violations—the vast majority of which were expressly excused by the state-issued and EPA-approved consent order of 1991. As was its custom, the EPA informed neither Virginia nor Smithfield about its pending action. Instead, the agency announced the news by leaking the story to *The Washington Post.*

I hoped other Virginians were asking the same questions I was. "Why did EPA surprise Virginia by secretly taking enforcement action...when it has known and acquiesced in the results-driven actions Virginia has taken against [Smithfield] since 1991? And why did EPA take this action after Virginia complied with a request from EPA, Justice, and the FBI to delay our civil action, so as not to jeopardize a criminal investigation?" And why, if the EPA estimated there had been 20,000 instances in the previous year when it could have overridden states, had it chosen to do so only four times—one in Virginia? Was it cynical to believe "there is some selection process" going on?

Hopkins told me privately that he had been told informally by EPA staff that the action was ordered by McCabe for political reasons and that the EPA's own enforcement staff had objected but been overruled.

Browner seemed to confirm that the EPA's agenda was political in remarks she made in a December 15 article in *The New York Times* article. Browner claimed that a "number of states that are emboldened by the anti-environmental sentiment that began here in Congress...are retreating from their commitment to enforce the law." But all the trouble-making states she mentioned had Republican governors—a point not lost on the Environmental Council of the States—who wrote to Browner in response:

> States are very concerned about what appears to be a retreat on your part from the partnership relation which had been carefully and, in some instances, painfully built over the past four years. State commissioners, some of whom have worked very hard to advance EPA's interests and agenda over the past few years, and to create and administer strong state

programs, are disappointed to be the objects of your apparent lack of trust.

We are particularly concerned that the comments you are alleged to have made have a strong partisan flavor. We note that the states mentioned throughout the report all have Republican governors...Clean air, clean water, and proper handling of waste material should not be—and must not become—political partisan issues.

One man who was adamant that the actions of the Allen Administration were not political was Smithfield chairman Luter, who was incredulous at suggestions that he received favorable treatment for having contributed to Allen's PAC. Luter had met Allen only once, he said, not spoken to him since Smithfield's troubles surfaced, and "our [company's] relationship with the Virginia DEQ has been very combative.

"I knew from the outset that these contributions would be public knowledge," Luter said. "Smithfield Foods has never asked for nor gotten any special favors from the Commonwealth since those contributions were made. In fact, just the opposite might be said. The Commonwealth has sued Smithfield Foods for millions in civil penalties."

On December 20, both *The Washington Post* and *The New York Times* published pro-EPA editorials, suggesting editorial boards were being lobbied by EPA flacks. The *Times* editors acknowledged that the agency was acting out of personal animus. "Carol Browner decided that she had been ignored and insulted by the Commonwealth of Virginia long enough," wrote the nation's paper of record. "Though the action was directed at the company, it was also a stinging rebuke to the Virginia state government."

A few weeks later, the *Post* published my letter responding to its editorial. It caught the eye of a Washington lawyer, Gary Baise, who wrote to tell me of his own recent experience. His client, Florida Cities Water Company had been the object of state enforcement action on relatively minor violations until the Department of Justice, "lacking a sufficient number of cases, took

this case on and sought $104 million in fines against my client."
The judge awarded only $309,000—a major victory over the EPA,
Baise noted.

Baise, however, was not your typical anti-big government
lawyer. He had helped to put together the EPA in 1970. What he
had learned "having worked on environmental matters for the
[p]ast 25 years," he told me, "is that the agency is becoming
politicized to the extent that it is not using good judgment with
respect to its enforcement cases. It would rather garner headlines
than improve environmental quality.

"This action just shows an EPA and Department of Justice
out of control with respect to these issues..."

I wrote him back, thanking him for the encouragement.
"The Commonwealth's approach to environmental policy focuses
on solutions to problems and compliance from businesses and
municipalities. State officials develop and implement unique,
innovative solutions that seek to ensure improvement in the quality
of our environment, as well as in our ability to respond to the needs
of our citizens. As a result, Virginia's natural resources are cleaner
and safer, and they are getting cleaner still."

"Positive results like these dishearten the EPA. It knows
that the states are better able to assist citizens and communities on
the environment without EPA intervention, and it doesn't like it."

In a twist of official contradiction to the claim that Virginia
was soft on polluters, John Smeltzer of the Justice Department
wrote a thank-you note to Frank Daniel, a Regional Director at the
DEQ.

> I am writing to thank you and the other employees at
> the Department of Environmental Quality who assisted the
> Department of Justice in the recently completed criminal
> prosecution of Terry L. Rettig. As you know, on January 16,
> 1997, Rettig was sentenced to thirty months in prison...one of
> the longest imposed in the country. This sentence stands as a
> testament not only to the widespread and egregious nature of
> Rettig's conduct, but also to the hard work and dedication of

the many inspectors and enforcement personnel who helped to bring this conduct to light.

Deserving special commendation is investigator Ralph Mayer, who prompted the federal investigation with an extremely thorough report and referral, and who continued to provide important insight and assistance throughout the prosecution.... Without the assistance of these and other DEQ employees, this prosecution would not have been possible.

On August 8, 1997, a federal district judge rejected the chance to assess Smithfield a staggering $174 million in fines, ordering the company to pay only $12.6 million for water-pollution violations. The EPA successfully claimed it was entitled to sue even though nearly three-fourths of the violations had been committed with the 1991 blessing of Virginia state officials and the EPA's approval because the consent order lacked firm deadlines and penalties—objections it did not voice to the Allen administration until 1996 with a presidential election looming on the horizon.

I believed that presidential politics accounted for much of the EPA's initial decision to take federal action against Smithfield. Bill Clinton was within two points of Bob Dole in Virginia, and the EPA and Justice Department had become so politicized under Clinton that they thought they could win votes for Clinton by trying to make it seem to Virginians that Republicans don't care about the environment. But even I was shocked by being used for mileage in my own state's gubernatorial race.

Two days after the Smithfield decision was handed down, Don Beyer, the Democratic candidate for governor, criticized the involvement of his opponent, Attorney General James Gilmore, in the Smithfield case. "Smithfield was finally held accountable," Beyer whined. "But it wasn't Virginia that held them accountable—not the attorney general—but the federal government, because we wouldn't do the job." This was a breathtakingly disingenuous statement, considering Smithfield was operating under a consent order arranged while Beyer was Lt. Governor.

"Politics, not preservation, has been the watchword of our Department of Environmental Quality," Beyer repeated at stops around the state. Yet the Wilder-Beyer Administration had engineered the consent order allowing Smithfield to dump excessive amounts of phosphorous in the Pagan River for what they believed was good reason: to keep the company from moving out of the state and taking 3,000 jobs with it.

Furthermore, Beyer promised, if elected he would replace both Hopkins and me—a gratuitous swipe at both of us, because neither would be expected to stay in any new administration. Gilmore disappointed many by proving equally eager to step over me on his way to the Executive Mansion. He tried to placate extremists by announcing he would not reappoint me, either.

The Lieutenant Governor stepped up the attacks. The state's pollution case against Smithfield Foods was "the greatest embarrassment of this Administration," he claimed, while continuing to refuse any responsibility for the Wilder-Beyer consent order. Rather, Beyer was convinced he was on the right track politically.

The environment, he said, "is a big issue for me." He added: "It'll probably be one of the two or three issues that helps me win this election."

Beyer was rejected resoundingly by Virginia voters in November 1997.

The sad postscript to this case was written as this book went to press. A report appeared in *The Washington Post* on October 3, 2000, on page B3 of the Metro Section.

> A record $12.6 million fine levied against Virginia's Smithfield Foods will stand because the U.S. Supreme Court rejected the pork-processing company's appeal yesterday without comment.
> The decision brings to a close the long-running fight over protecting the Pagan River from processing waste. The

Environmental Protection Agency sued Smithfield, contending that the company violated its pollution permits thousands of times from 1991 to 1997 and that state regulators failed to protect the river.

Smithfield's attorneys argued that the company was unfairly caught in a power play between federal and state regulators. Virginia officials had agreed in 1991 not to fine the company for discharging phosphorus as long as Smithfield promised to hook up to a regional sewer system. When a federal judge imposed the $12.6 million fine in 1997, it was the largest ever under the Clean Water Act.

The hard lesson of this case is that states really do not have the authority to resolve difficult cases in ways they deem best for their citizens and their environment. Governor Wilder and the Water Board that served in 1991 made a difficult decision, one that Governor Allen's team chose not to revisit but to enforce. The federal Environmental Protection Agency that had uttered no objection to the 1991 consent order chose to make a political issue out of the matter in 1996 seeking political advantage for their presidential candidate.

The *Post* reported the facts regarding the consent order. But, make no mistake about it. In the Clinton-Gore years, there was no state and no consent order that could escape the political attack of EPA if their chosen candidates needed an environmental issue to rally votes.

6. Natural resourcefulness

Unintentionally, environmental politics may have inculcated an essentially negative approach towards natural resources. There is a "gotcha" character to some strains of environmentalism, a kind of obsession with spectacular scandals and harsh sanctions for evil polluters. This is not to say that bad behavior should go unpunished. Caring for our environment, however, ought to be a happy and positive endeavor—an effort not merely to combat the destructive, but to promote and celebrate what is good.

Temperamentally, George Allen's environmentalism had an optimistic, human character. He certainly thought about the need to block wrongdoers, but he was also focused on promoting the good. I not only found this brand of husbandry attractive as a philosophy and a personal approach, but a highly practical one as well. The natural resources God has provided, we may be grateful, are resilient. Even when damaged, ecosystems are responsive to good management, and can, like individual plants and animals, rebound and repair themselves with proper care. Some of the most powerful human tools, from soil conservation to new kinds of pest control, involve putting the forces of nature to work for themselves.

Essentially, Governor Allen was an environmental populist. He believed that the goal of policy was to enable people to behave voluntarily in environmentally sound ways. Far from seeing people as the problem, as some groups did, he saw people as our most precious resource of all. Their ingenuity, inventiveness, and basic goodness, in Allen's eyes, were all potent forces to be shaped.

I shared George Allen's view of natural resources and of people and was determined not to be merely a pollution fighter—I wanted to be an environmental protector, indeed, a builder and improver. Accordingly, even though I naturally had to spend some of my time dealing with polluters, I thought it would be wrong to ignore all the positive opportunities for improving our resource base in Virginia. I tried instead to balance some time every day working with the people in my departments to develop their ideas and to focus on positive resource management. I'm convinced, looking back on it, that these seemingly humble initiatives may have been some of the most important things we did for Virginia.

Greg Crist's work to put Virginia prison inmates to work on environmental projects was just one example. Crist was on a track so fast he nearly left smoke in his wake. He had just finished college at William & Mary and was working on Capitol Square as a Governor's Fellow assigned to work for me. Initially, I think, he found me demanding; I expected a lot, and we were at the center of many policy battles. But I went out of my way to make Crist part of the team, and he seemed to appreciate that.

When Crist came to work with such obvious talent, I decided he could handle, and would thrive under, a challenging assignment. Within days of his arrival, Crist was sitting at his desk not far from my office when I walked out with a big stack of folders. On top was Governor Allen's State of the Commonwealth speech, and I called it to Crist's attention.

"The Governor made it clear in this speech that we can tap inmate labor to help improve our natural resources," I said. "Your job is to develop a program and here are some research papers from various governments and think tanks to help you do that."

Governor Allen realized that one of the signature legislative achievements of his Administration—the abolition of parole—would mean more inmates staying behind bars longer. Prisoners would need something constructive to do. Helping to clean up the state they had polluted with criminality was poetically just. The project was to be a joint endeavor between the secretariats of Natural Resources and Public Safety. I had the work that needed to be done; Public Safety Secretary Jerry Kilgore had the prisoners.

So with Jeff Wilson, his counterpart in Kilgore's office, Crist began studying similar programs in other states. After concluding that Minnesota's Sentenced to Serve program, which allowed judges to impose community service on criminals convicted of non-violent crimes, was a worthy model, Crist and Wilson went to Minnesota to see the program first-hand.

The Minnesota director explained its workings to them and drove them around to visit various sites, where the Virginia gentlemen watched convicts peeling paint to prepare a building for refurbishing, sandblasting graffiti off buildings in downtown Minneapolis, and digging fence post holes. Talking to Minnesota's inmates, Crist and Wilson were surprised to learn that the prisoners generally appreciated the chance to be productive. Apparently, they greatly preferred being sentenced to serve than being sentenced to interminable boredom behind bars.

Returning to Virginia, Crist and Wilson went to work tailoring the plan to the Commonwealth in light of two principal differences: Minnesota's program was not geared toward environmental improvement as Virginia's would be, and officers there did not carry guns. Minnesota found it unnecessary to arm security guards because the program's participants were usually serving short sentences, often in local jails. Virginia would be drawing from the state's prisons, a more hardened population. Kilgore and I agreed: We have to arm the guards. With an experiment like this, we must assure the citizens they are safe.

Virginia also wanted its program to be voluntary, which Crist had doubts about, but found to his surprise that Virginia's prisoners also welcomed the chance to work. "This project made sense not only for taxpayers," Crist said later, "but had a tremendous rehabilitative factor that you can't quantify."

A Virginia prison official told him the same thing when Crist asked, "What do you think?"

"What folks need to realize," the warden explained, "is that these guys are going to get out, they are going back to society. And if you can't trust them to mow the grass or clean up a community center, how can you expect them to go back and be productive citizens in society?"

The nuts and bolts work was to link inmates with environmental projects, and Crist had a clever idea. Sitting down with a map of Virginia, he marked the locations of the state's minimum-security prisons and then went back and marked the environmental targets—tire piles, state parks, tributaries, oyster reefs, landfills, historic sites, etc.—making it easy to assign workers to the most convenient project.

Crist also called my department heads and asked, "Can you help me with any ideas?" Bill Pruitt, Commissioner of the Virginia Marine Resources Commission said, "We need some artificial oyster-bed reefs." The Department of Historic Resources knew of old buildings that needed painting. State park officials had screens, trails, parking lots and picnic tables in need of repair. DEQ said it could use a hand cleaning up old tire piles. One of my projects was riparian buffers, and inmates planted trees along rivers.

Convicted Offenders Serving Virginia, or ConServ Virginia, as it came to be known, expanded quickly, making inmate labor available to localities as well. As long as local officials were willing to pay for transporting and guarding inmates, the rest was arranged by the state.

It is difficult to imagine that anyone could criticize such a common-sense notion as inmates working to earn their keep. But those who reflexively criticized the Allen Administration finally came up with a reason: The usual suspects complained that ConServ Virginia would take jobs out of the private sector. That was a specious argument, Crist tried to explain, because inmates were doing jobs the private sector wasn't interested in, and the government didn't have as priorities at the time.

In retrospect, the speed with which ConServ Virginia was developed surprised even me. Crist's started work in June and the program was kicked off in November. Crist later explained to a researcher: "With the flexibility Dunlop and Kilgore gave us—and the flexibility the Governor gave them—we could really develop a program in some uncharted areas," he said. It was a good demonstration—as if I needed more—that finding good people and letting them do their jobs is the center of an effective organization.

In the late 1980s, environmentalist Paddy Katzen headed a committee to beautify Fauquier County in Northern Virginia. After that, she began a grass-roots campaign to promote recycling there. Katzen worked as a volunteer; now Recycling Coordinator is a paid position. "She was a real go-getter," says her successor, Benji Brackman.

In 1994 Katzen joined our Administration part-time, working on various projects and specific DEQ issues about which I had concerns. She did for me what she had done for her county: scouted innovative environmental remedies. Katzen was particularly interested in the emerging technology of bioremediation: the use of natural processes to treat environmental maladies.

While studying effective ways to cap landfills—a necessary step to keep rainwater from soaking into the buried garbage and leaching contaminants—Katzen learned about the work of Iowa professor Louis Licht. Dr. Licht had discovered that fast-growing poplar trees, when planted on top of landfills, could soak up rainfall and snow before the moisture seeps all the way down to the trash. The extensive root systems of the trees also go down deep, and absorb much of the leachate, preventing the pollutants from reaching waterways and groundwater. Not only is the landfill kept clean, but it yields a harvestable crop of trees.

Experimental projects using the "ecolotrees," as Licht called them, were underway in Iowa and Oregon, where they were functioning beyond all expectations. "Whatever we hoped these trees would do, they have done more," Licht said. "So it leads me to believe that these plants, if engineered and controlled, can achieve what we want."

After being briefed on this innovative idea, I was enthusiastic about testing it in Virginia. Katzen wrote a memo that formally proposed that Virginia study the feasibility of planting poplar trees at Alleghany County's Kim-Stan landfill, an abandoned landfill for which the Attorney General's office on Mary Sue Terry's watch was unable to nail the culprit. So, our administration was looking for remediation ideas.

"These hybrid poplars are a living pump and filter system that sucks up excess fertilizer and pollutants," Katzen explained. "They grow fast, provide a habitat, and help stop erosion." I was enthusiastic and approved the study—but not for Kim-Stan. That site was too large and troubled to risk experimentation and to raise peoples' hopes quite yet. Instead, the DEQ staff agreed to permit a test of the ecolotrees at a landfill in Charles City County.

"It's opening the door to a new way of thinking,"   Katzen said of the program. "What we want to suggest to these engineers is that they can use plants as one of their tools."

"The trees may be too good to be true," she conceded, "but wouldn't it be wonderful if it works?"

Well, not to everyone. For some of our opponents, there was a threefold problem. First, the idea hadn't been proposed by the federal government. Second, it relied on private funding. And third, if it worked, credit would go to the Allen Administration.

"You have to wonder if there's politics at play," grumbled Paul Schwartz of Clean Water Action. "How little can you get away with in terms of remediation?"

"We need to go slow," said Jason Gray of the Virginia Water Project in Roanoke, "and not just pass it off as a way for communities to save money in the short run so they don't have to put an impermeable cap over their landfill."

Such responses taxed the patience of many, including the *Roanoke Times & World News.* "In the final analysis, what counts is what works," editorialized the paper, which was hardly one of my biggest boosters.

"In the case of the aspen poplars, this can't be known until the idea is put to a fair and valid test. But if it does work, and it's cheaper, that means it's better. And environmentalists should be the first to celebrate. They too often ignore a basic inference from economics: that if you reduce the cost of environmental protection, it's more likely to get done."

I was especially happy that the effort not only got off the ground, but that it did so primarily because of the initiative of an environmentalist like Paddy Katzen who found solutions for real challenges. Government needs more of such citizenship and voluntarism at its core, and it needs to do more to make sure it encourages such efforts. We were fortunate in Virginia as it seemed we were teeming with such activity.

Today, the test at Charles City County continues with 11 acres of tree caps. Lee Wilson, manager of the site, reports that visually, the site looks good but they have experienced some technical challenges. A drought the first year, an insect infestation, a hurricane blow-down, some highly intensive maintenance required, and this year, daily rain, have all contributed to questions as to whether the technical performance will merit long term continuation of the project. An additional test is being conducted in Fauquier County where a farmer grows poplars as a streamside buffer and hopes that they will also become a cash crop for him. This site is doing very well.

Meanwhile "ecolotree" landfill projects are now being sponsored by none other than EPA in Georgia and Iowa, according to Dr. Robert Schnabel, an associate of Dr. Licht's. Pennsylvania also has a new "ecolotree" site that was established in 1998. Virginia was on the cutting edge of the idea of using "trees as tools" as Paddy Katzen would say.

Instead of promoting environmentalism for one day a year, for example, as in the popular "Earth Day" celebrations, Governor Allen and I instituted Operation Spruce-Up in 1995, during which the state encouraged activities that would improve the environment over an entire month. Its purpose was to promote, recognize, and reward voluntary stewardship among Virginians, and it succeeded. Students at Appomattox Elementary School sponsored an Adopt-an-Eagle program. Boy Scouts in Chester built wooden duck boxes for Presquile National Wildlife Refuge. Members of the local 4-H Club planted pine seedlings in Halifax. Virginia Military Institute cadets cleaned illegal dumps and repaired hiking trails. And the Professional Paddlesports Association cleaned up river-access areas. The two state employees who directed the Operation Spruce-Up programs during the Allen administration, Carol Comstock and Bonnie Phillips, reported increasing success each year with more citizen participation across the state. More student groups, civic associations, scout troops and Virginia companies participated and sponsored Spruce-Ups each year.

Under a program we championed at DCR, "Friends of the Parks," volunteerism at state parks increased to more than 100,000 hours. Not only did the programs do good work, they fostered a spirit of ownership and care for the environment that invigorated citizens across the whole state to become "Friends of the Parks."

Not everyone, of course, was enthusiastic. When I invited the Virginia chapter of the Sierra Club to participate in the "Friends of the Parks" program, Chairman Tyla Matteson declined on behalf of the group, stating the Sierra Club's disapproval of my policies. "Some of the activities you suggest to entice park supporters are those that should be provided by experienced park rangers educated in the natural sciences," Matteson sniffed. Worse, from the club's perspective, "it is assumed that the savings are being diverted to other state programs and are being used to attract industry to the state." Actually, our main purpose was to improve the parks, but I have to admit, if all this positive commotion involving Virginia citizens being good stewards of our natural resources attracted some investor or high tech entrepreneur or library or any other business activity to Virginia, I couldn't be more pleased.

My husband George and I, along with our little dog Maggie, traveled constantly during Operation Spruce-Up to work

104

side by side with fellow Virginians improving the environment of our state. From Montgomery County's Broomin' and Bloomin' to George Washington's Ferry Farm in Fredricksburg; and from Virginia Beach's First Landing State Park to a Hanover ball field working with Daisy Girl Scouts, we picked up, cleared out, and planted.

Kathleen Lawrence, the Director of the Department of Conservation and Recreation, and I traveled to "Friends of the Parks" events from First Landing in Tidewater to Pocahontas, Douthat, and Leesylvania, on to Natural Tunnel in Southwest Virginia and many parks in between. At each park we visited, we spent time talking to Virginians about our vision of citizen "ownership" of the parks. Kathleen recounted one comment after the event at Natural Tunnel, "The people here are so excited that Governor Allen has expanded the purpose of the new park facilities. Instead of just an environmental education center, they have a community center that is an invitation for all the citizens to use, enjoy and care for the park. They really want this park to be an important part of their community." Our view, exactly!

In addition to spring renewal of our natural resources, we were also seeing renewal of the spirit of Virginia stewardship. It was an inspiration.

Fish, salt-water and fresh water, were the focus of Allen Administration initiatives too. Two separate agencies in my secretariat had primary responsibility for the fisheries. The Virginia Marine Resources Commission oversaw the state's salt-water fisheries and the Department of Game and Inland Fisheries has the same responsibility for fresh water fisheries. The agencies worked together often but the challenges and constituencies were really quite different.

One initiative both agencies invested in that Governor Allen particularly liked was the fish passage at Bosher's Dam. This was the last major block to migrating fish on the James River.

Both the VMRC and DGIF constituencies had an interest in this project, too, as the American Shad, Hickory Shad, Alewives and Blueback Herring would return to their historic spawning grounds once the fish passage was completed.

One rainy morning, Bill Woodfin, Director of the Department of Game and Inland Fisheries, and I headed out of Richmond to meet DGIF staff just above Bosher's Dam to stock millions of marked shad fry in the James River. It sounds like a challenging project but the truth be told, we had giant fish tanks on trucks and our job was to open the spigot at the right time to flood the upper James with tiny, tiny, tiny fish. These fish would mature, make their way to the ocean from this spot in the upper James and return here to spawn, we hoped. With the completion of the fish ladder, the likelihood of success was great. This passageway would open over 140 river miles of additional spawning habitat. The markings the fishery biologists used on the shad fry would allow them to measure the success of the program when they examined spawning fish in later years.

A private organization headed the fundraising drive for the fishway at Bosher's. Governor Allen and I both supported this initiative and personally contributed to the James River Association's funding drive. It meant that people were taking ownership in this project and that was good. Patricia Jackson, Director of the James River Association, Bill Woodfin and I all manned shovels the day we broke ground to begin construction on this vertical slot fishway in July 1997. The state and federal governments invested along with hundreds of private citizens to build a fish ladder that would benefit fisheries and provide a wonderful opportunity for science education for Virginians, young and old. And, it was commercial fishermen who captured spawning fish for the shad restoration program. This was just one example of private initiatives throughout Virginia that the Allen Administration was proud to promote and support with state assistance.

Two other fisheries programs captured my attention as areas for positive reform. One was opening day of trout season.

As popular as it was, and it was popular, congregating thousands of Virginia anglers in trout streams and lakes on one day each year had negative impacts on natural resources. Sure it was a celebration of spring for many anglers. But, the resulting streambank erosion, issues of water quality in trout streams, stocking operations, and hatchery management issues made the idea of changing to a year round program very attractive.

But change is always difficult. The Department of Game and Inland Fisheries has the most active and involved constituency of any government agency, so the staff was careful to talk to their trout fishermen and other constituencies about eliminating "opening day," and going to a year-round season instead. Nearly 100,000 anglers buy trout-fishing permits annually. And, of course, there are many small mom and pop shops that have booming business on opening day. We talked to them also explaining that without an opening day, there might not be such a big business on any one day, but anglers would likely be visiting their area more often throughout the year and the change would be good for all the resources. Not everyone agreed with the proposal, but the DGIF staff did a great job in outlining the merits and taking into consideration the dissenters' concerns.

The Board approved a year round season. Now, DGIF can manage its hatcheries more efficiently, regularly stock the streams and lakes and provide trout fishermen with challenging sport throughout the year.

The second fisheries program I was interested in studying for reform was the commercial rockfish (striped bass) program. The Virginia Marine Resources Commission manages this program. Rockfish have rebounded to record numbers since the low point twenty years ago and are favorites of many fishermen. Maintaining a healthy population is important for many reasons and one of them is that Virginia has been able to increase its quota to 1,700,000 pounds per annum as the fishery recovered. My plan was to put in place Virginia's first Individual Transferable Quota Program for this commercial fishery. This ITQ Program would put in place elements of private property ownership and stewardship for this fishery. A waterman would know that he "owned" a right to a specified portion of the annual quota. He would have a self-interest in preserving and maintaining the value of his property and would be an advocate for sound fishery management.

Bill Pruitt, Commissioner of the VMRC, and Jack Travelstead, the top fisheries scientist, and I had many discussions with watermen who were concerned about this change. I visited with watermen where they worked and lived; Tangier Island, the Eastern Shore, in Mathews, Gloucester, Middlesex, Lancaster, and Northumberland Counties. Rising at three or four a.m., on the Bay by five a.m., this is typical of a Virginia's waterman's day. While many often came to see me in Richmond, I respected them and their work and met many of them on their home turf to discuss these issues.

Watermen are the fishermen who fish for a living so you and I who live in Northern Virginia or Norfolk or Roanoke or other Virginia towns—and even Washington, D.C.—and work at different jobs can still enjoy a nice rockfish dinner at a local restaurant or buy some fresh fish at Ukrop's or Giant Food or a local fish market. Virginia's watermen work to provide for us who have neither the time, nor the fishing vessels nor the stamina to catch our own fresh seafood.

Watermen, like many Virginians, are concerned about change and so they were with this new idea of Individually Transferable Quotas. They might well like an idea but they see the potential for government to go from a good idea to more regulation, more taxes and more government faster than you could put bait on a hook. Bill, Jack and I persuaded them that ITQs are a good idea that would likely result in less government interference and put them more in charge of their work and their own assets.

We explained that by owning an ITQ, fishermen in the striped bass fishery could end wasteful fishing practices since they could now be assured of not losing the opportunity to catch their entire quota. They could sell their ITQ to another fisherman. In other words, each waterman could manage his percentage of the quota in a way that benefits him and his long-term investment in "his" fishery resource, equipment, manpower and government fees. The Virginia Marine Resources Board, a citizen board appointed by the Governor, approved the plan and our staff implemented it. Today, the program is working. Certainly, the program could have gone further to establish a program like those that flourished in New Zealand and Australia, but Virginia's program is working, proving the idea for those who follow. The flounder fishery is one that could easily accommodate such a program as well. This is the future for sustainable fisheries, private sector watermen or commercial fishermen and Virginia is helping to lead the way.

Because a single truck tire contains nine quarts of oil, piles of them create fire hazards—while also providing breeding grounds for mosquitoes, rats, and other vermin harmful to public health and safety. The problem is, there are limited ways to dispose of tires.

At the beginning of my term, I was given a briefing book describing the state's environmental problems. Near the top of the list: almost 18 million old tires cluttering Virginia's landscape. Lawmakers thought they had addressed the problem several years earlier by adding a 50 cent tax on new tires to create a fund to pay for the disposal of old ones. But I soon learned the money was merely accumulating in state coffers. The policy when the Allen Administration took office seemed to be less concerned with actually solving the environmental problem than with engineering social behavior. The largest payouts were proposed not to people who disposed of the most tires, but to those who came up with the most creative ways to recycle used tires. In only a few years, the fund had grown to nearly $6 million. And the tire piles were growing, not shrinking.

It seemed to me that this was hardly the original intent of the law. What mattered was that the tires were gone, not whether they were made into sandals. Under my guidance, Peter Schmidt and one of his deputies at DEQ revised the program to reward elimination of waste tires rather than industrial policy initiatives. Suddenly old tires began disappearing faster than shrimp on an all-you-can-eat buffet. Where few had been disposed of previously, tires began vanishing by the millions. Over four million tires were recycled and the most hazardous piles were cleaned up.

It was gratifying to see the citizen efforts that flourished under the new policy. A Richmond company earned $200,000 for compressing nearly half a million tires into one-ton bales to filter run-off at a hog farm. Citizens in some communities were offered amnesty to bring tires into the dump on certain days for shredding, with each household allowed to dispose of up to 50 tires. (Shredded tires can be used as a drainage device in place of rock, provide ground cover for play grounds, and become part of the mix that makes asphalt.) A South Carolina septic company took some of the scrap tires to create drainage fields in mobile home parks. A North Carolina company built a golf course on bales of scrap tires it hauled from Virginia. Waste to energy plants used tire shred as fuel to burn garbage and landfills mixed shred with dirt to cover the day's influx of trash.

Only a few years earlier, the tire fund had paid simply to build a fence around one pile.

Moreover, the Governor decided to institutionalize improvement. He proposed a bill, and in 1996 signed it into law, holding landowners responsible for damage to adjacent land if tires in a pile of 50,000 or more catch fire.

"It's consistent with our environmental policy, which is that people should be responsible for their actions," Allen said. "Everything we try to do is based on common sense, sound science, and market approaches."

As contradictory as it seems to some, hunters are good conservationists. They contribute millions from license fees each year, and even more millions from taxes on hunting equipment. Additionally, hunters typically obey hunting laws, respect other people's property, and don't litter or degrade the land.

I saw hunters as natural allies. They are interested in having a good hunting experience. And I wanted to take advantage of that wholesome desire, and of their expertise. I knew we could encourage hunters to take on some specific tasks that would help improve the habitat for game, and accomplishing that improves habitat for other critters, too.

Quail Unlimited worked with Virginia Power for years to plant under overhead power lines that would be attractive to quail. I walked with officials of both organizations through areas in Southside Virginia they had planted, happy to encourage and celebrate their stewardship. Or take the Wild Turkey Federation, which had worked tirelessly to assure that Virginia's wild turkey population is healthier now than when Jamestown was settled. The organization was also very active training young people—"Jakes," they called them—on good hunting ethics and skills. I went to their events as often as I possibly could to show appreciation for their commitment to Virginia's resources.

Governor Allen and I also boosted Hunters for the Hungry, a great organization in his view and mine. It takes donated deer, which it trims, dresses and then donates to needy families around the state. And, its success is in large measure due to support and assistance from the Virginia Deer Hunters Association. My efforts did not go unnoticed. The Virginia Deer Hunters Association was pleased with what we were trying to accomplish. I was happy to attend fund-raisers, such as the Virginia Big Game Contest, that my predecessors, whose greatest interest was the role of government, had not. When I came under fire from environmental activists groups, it turned out that I had vigorous defenders among Virginia's sportsmen and outdoors people. And they have a defender in me.

Perhaps the greatest challenge I faced was to define and articulate an appropriate role for the Virginia Department of Historic Resources, one of the eight agencies in my secretariat. This would be an important opportunity in any state, but in Virginia, the task may almost be considered solemn. Virginia is steeped in history and its people take pride in the fact.

Many of the great and memorable events of the entire American experience have taken place in Virginia, and Virginians know and treasure this.

And yet, at the same time both the Governor and I were committed to reducing the size and reach of government bureaucracies as part of our commitment to promote economic development in the Commonwealth. I was convinced that there were innovative ways in which the agency could help Virginians, indeed all Americans, appreciate historic resources even more than ever, and at the same time contribute to the Virginia economic renaissance. Additionally, protection of private property rights as guaranteed under the Fifth Amendment of the U.S. Constitution was a very important priority for me in considering the operations of this agency. Ownership inspires stewardship if owners can be confident that the state will not preclude them from using their property in ways that enhance the quality of life for their families.

Over the years, the Department of Historic Resources had developed a reputation as an overbearing elite that advocated and sought to impose preservation of structures, battlefields, and the like regardless of historical significance, the cost to the citizens or interference with other people's private property. In fact, the broader preservation community had come to be somewhat oriented towards government-run, top-down efforts in its thinking. The public, the activists feared, did not have sufficient reverence for historic resources. Without government, they worried, no one would preserve or care for these assets.

My goal was to encourage good stewardship of historic resources by the citizens while reorienting the agency to one that served all the citizens. I believed it was important to foster the idea that historic resources can be valuable and have economic, educational, and social as well as ascetic benefits for their owners, and, indeed, for the communities in which they are located. The Allen Administration wanted to demonstrate that there are alternatives to government control and direction of every aspect of human endeavor that actually work best—including that which is best for historic resources. In short, we wanted a DHR that would work with Virginia citizens as a helpful servant to encourage conservation and preservation of historic resources.

The first stop on this trek was personnel. We needed to recruit people who had a demonstrated concern for Virginia's history and its historic treasures, and yet who shared Governor Allen's conviction that the department's mission was to benefit all Virginians. I was looking for a unique individual, a person who had demonstrated a love and respect for history, particularly Virginia's heritage.

One candidate came by way of a memo handed to me by Frank Atkinson, counselor to the Governor. He commented that while he didn't know where I was with respect to historic resources, if I thought the ideas in the paper would be useful, he knew the author and would be happy to put us in touch. Well, as they say, the rest is history.

I studied the paper carefully. It was exactly what I was looking for...a thoughtful and creative plan that would implement my vision of what a wonderful opportunity we had to reform the historic resources movement in Virginia.

It was based on the principles that the people are our most valuable natural resource and would respond positively to incentive-based, voluntary, and cooperative-oriented leadership; that a growing economy and an improving environment—even the environment of historic resources—go hand in hand. Governor Allen's success in attracting economic development and expanding Virginia's economy would directly affect our success in this initiative and the department's reforms would directly affect the Governor's success.

The meeting between the Virginia attorney who had written the memo, H. Alexander Wise Jr., and me occurred on a bright sunny afternoon. It was my special delight to learn that Alex had served in the Reagan administration in a position that had required the same kind of creative thinking, commitment to conservative principles and policy goals while facing an uncertain relationship with the affected constituencies. He persevered then and was successful. An additional element that demonstrated his likelihood for success at this task was that he was just then wrapping up the VMI lawsuit in which he had been a member of the legal team in his position with McGuire, Woods, Battle and Boothe. His firm had defended VMI against the federal government's intrusive meddling and litigations. This also impressed me.

I shared the paper Wise had prepared with Governor Allen and recommended to the Governor that he appoint Alex as director of the Department of Historic Resources. He did so. Alex became Director of the Department in June of 1994.

Additionally, I recruited a professional for my personal Secretariat staff who had spent part of her career at the U.S. Department of the Interior. It is in this federal department that the core activity for historic resources is located. Kathleen Kilpatrick had the experience and professional contacts to help in dealing with that federal minefield and the wherewithal not to be intimidated by federal bureaucrats who might be inclined to lord their power over Virginia since we intended to march to a different drummer on this front. She also had a strong commitment to the history of our country and its resources and an understanding that economic growth and development in the Commonwealth could benefit Virginia's history and her historic resources.

Her role with DHR (and the Departments of Game and Inland Fisheries, Conservation and Recreation, and the Marine Resources Commission) was to monitor the agency, advise me of potential problems as they arose, handle the flow of routine communication and mail from my office to the agency. She had the authority to work closely with Alex and agency personnel on the Administration initiatives and was a key member of the management team that developed those initiatives. She was my confidante and closest adviser on policy and management matters relating to historic resources.

Our study of the department's operations revealed that the Department of Historic Resources had one satellite office, in Roanoke, which had been instrumental in renovating that city's historic downtown. The staff were known for their helpful attitude and expertise, and the office was well regarded in the community—it was the kind of partnership that was win-win. Believing, as did Thomas Jefferson—and George Allen—that government closest to people governed best, my aim in all agencies was to have the offices and the people in the communities across Virginia rather than congregated in Richmond. The Roanoke office seemed like a good mode on which to build.

Alex Wise and the historic resources team responded to the challenge and developed a creative plan that drew upon the concepts that historic resources can and should be assets to individuals and communities. Their proposal drew upon the view that if local governments understood and believed this premise, if the state demonstrated through deed that it really wanted to serve the communities and the people, then these communities would compete to become strategic partners with the Commonwealth and host communities for field offices of the department.

The plan divided the state into four regions and sent out requests for proposals that said in effect, "We will provide the staff and expertise. What will you contribute to the partnership?" With the Roanoke office ensconced in property owned by the city making them the strategic partner in that region, three regional offices remained to be designated. Competing bids came in for every regional office—some offered office space, voice mail, utilities, and clerical assistance. The offers were reviewed by Wise and his management team and then reviewed with me. In every instance, there was an eager partner who understood the partnership that the state offered would be a boon to their community and indeed their region of the state.

The first location chosen for a new field office was in Winchester. Governor George Allen and I, along with hundreds of citizens, participated in the ceremony that took the historic resources offices out to be with the people, to help them make their resources work for their communities. The competition continued and other field offices were established in partnership with Petersburg and Portsmouth. The Winchester office has since moved to Frederick County.

I attended every opening ceremony and visited the Roanoke office because I wanted the entire staff of DHR and the citizens to know that the Governor and I enthusiastically supported this initiative and that the initiative was based on certain Administration principles that guided these decisions. At the opening of one regional office in December 1996, I elaborated on the decision.

"One of the hallmarks of this Administration is a commitment to improve services to Virginians," I said. "Governor Allen knows that public servants must be out among the people they serve. We also know that Virginia is much more than Richmond; it is all of Virginia and all of her people. For these reasons, we are decentralizing state government—moving public servants out of Richmond and into communities where they will work directly with citizens."

Wise began moving employees from Richmond into the field offices where their new responsibility was to demonstrate that historic resources could be more of an asset than a burden. He did not face significant resistance from his employees, though there were some that expressed uncertainty about the decentralization move to be sure. For many, however, a move offered personal and professional rejuvenation. In the field, they could work directly with the historic resources, see and know the properties. They also would make much more effective sales representatives if they were part of the community and not a nameless faceless bureaucrat telling people what to do with their property.

But we did encounter opposition from the usual suspects opposed to any weakening of central control. Many in the preservation community chose to misrepresent, and others simply misinterpreted, the action as Governor Allen's attempt to "gut history." What they really feared, Wise believed, was losing what they perceived as the critical mass inherent in a central agency. I agreed with him.

"People who don't have a lot of confidence in being able to market their ideas think they have more leverage if there's one group in a central location to deal with," I surmised. "They believe that using the power of government is necessary to advance their ideas. We just reject that notion and believe good ideas will be successful if you work with the people...it is another way in which we apply the notion George Washington advanced that government should be a helpful servant, not a fearsome master."

As the decentralization plan was being developed and proceeding, other reform programs were also advancing. The core element around which our various initiatives were organized was dubbed the "Virginia History Initiative." One description of this plan was a sort of Marshall Plan for the state's museums. "We can give them the confidence to stand on their own two legs," Wise had told the Governor. "They can pool resources by working together instead of expecting everything to come from the government."

The Virginia History Initiative was launched with its first formal meeting in January of 1996. The Department of Historic Resources assembled dozens of leaders from across Virginia, from large and small organizations, from those committed to preservation, interpretation and use of history assets for public and private benefit, from local and state government and from the business community. As Alex Wise stated, "this is a citizen-driven, bipartisan, voluntary effort." Ninety-three Virginians attended as participants and none were observers. Indeed, everyone made substantial contributions to the final product.

Governor Allen publicly unveiled the initiative at a ceremony in historic downtown Fredericksburg in July 1995. He received the final report in a public ceremony at the Virginia Historical Society in January 1998. The entire project was aimed at promoting Virginia history in such a way as to excite Virginians and their visitors about our rich heritage, to promote cooperation amongst all history museums and historic sites and thereby enhance heritage tourism, and to strengthen the stewardship ethic in the communities across Virginia.

As in other areas, much of our historic resources effort focused on encouraging Virginians to take action themselves. One such policy was the enactment of a tax credit program to spur private investment in the renovation of historic buildings. The credit for introduction of a legislative proposal goes to the Preservation Alliance of Virginia, a private group that arranged for a legislator to put the bill in the hopper. But my department played a critical role in shepherding the concept safely through the legislative process. A tireless legislative liaison, Kathleen Kilpatrick developed environmental and economic impact data, provided testimony and took the lead in working behind the scenes to secure Republican support for a bill that reflected our commitment to enable private initiative. Governor Allen signed the bill proudly and thanked me personally for our team's aggressive work to put in place a potent tool for preservation.

Similarly, the Allen Administration made a concerted effort to ensure that property owners were aware of their rights under the state and federal preservation laws. To some of our friends in the historical community, this was anathema, arming what they saw as recalcitrant taxpayers with information to resist the necessary strong hand of government in shielding history. But Governor Allen was convinced that people would be reasonable if they were reassured that their property was not going to be taken, or regulated capriciously—and they could then be encouraged to take preservation initiatives of their own volition, without being ordered to do so. Furthermore, it was their right to enjoy the full protection of the laws.

Here again was the quintessence of what we sought to achieve in so many other areas of resource management—the concept of servant leadership and a populist faith in people. Kathleen Kilpatrick, then the Deputy Director of our Department of Historic Resources, put it very well in a piece of testimony she delivered on behalf of the state before a House committee: "In Virginia, we have focused our efforts not on regulation and mandatory programs, but on providing leadership to encourage private stewardship of our historic resources. We believe that the proper role of government is to foster and support private stewardship efforts by offering guidance, technical assistance, recognition, and incentives to encourage private efforts, not to regulate for the sake of regulating."

Wise's most significant coup, perhaps, was his development of a novel remedy for the department's most pressing need: adequate space for the state's extensive collection of stored artifacts collected over many decades from thousands of sites. Governor Allen's Blue Ribbon Strike Force has expressed concern about the accessibility and security of the department's collections, information, and programs. The department's archaeological collection alone was comprised of more than 5 million objects spanning the earliest prehistoric periods to the 20th Century—the largest collection in the state. Yet the artifacts were housed in an old tobacco warehouse several blocks away from the offices, insufficiently protected and largely inaccessible. My counsel to those who worked under my direction was always to "think outside the box" when seeking solutions to challenges we faced. Wise's remedy demonstrated this kind of thinking. It was creative, cost effective, dramatic, and exactly the kind of ideas we should expect from Governor Allen's appointees.

When we went to the Governor to put the idea before him and seek his reaction before proceeding, his reaction was positive, with one rule. "Let's not add any public spending," he told Alex.

So Alex proceeded to call Charles Bryan, director of the private Virginia Historical Society, which had a wonderful facility in a prime Richmond location and a reputation for high-powered and effective fundraising. In the phone call, Alex suggested pooling collections to create a proper state history exhibit. He further suggested that "the land was available for a building expansion and the Department of Historic Resources staff could move to the new wing you build."

Of course, there would be many hurdles to cross in achieving such a goal, but we could see enormous benefits to the people and the historic resources of the Commonwealth. We were willing to pay the Historical Society the same rent the state charged the department for offices in three townhouses on Capitol Square. The state's employees and visitors would be better off in a new building at the Historical Society site on the corner of Boulevard and Kensington, where there would be ample parking and little reason to fear for their safety, compared to where they were downtown. By pooling resources, both historic groups could have a better facility and offer Virginians better services. For instance, a state of the art conservation lab could be built in the new wing and in such a way as to open this activity to student groups who could observe and learn about conservation techniques. And, the state's warehoused artifacts could be made available to scholars for research and to the public in a new Historical Society exhibit that would add new attractions to their already impressive material.

Bryan reacted the way most people would if asked to spend millions of dollars: Albeit politely, Alex reported that Bryan had made it clear he thought Alex's sanity was tenuous.

Wise, though, persisted. That fall, he invited Bryan and the Historical Society board to the warehouse to see the artifacts and, he hoped, to note their shabby surroundings and limited accessibility. The plan worked; Wise drew both interest and sympathy from board members. The society's collection told the story of how prominent Virginians had lived; the society had silver and portraits, costumes and writings from the Commonwealth's elite. But the department had in its possession the items that told the rest of the story—the sort of everyday trinkets used by ordinary people that they don't think enough of to save but that tell us so much. Unlike the Historical Society's collections, the state's artifacts could have belonged to slaves, yeoman farmers, Indians, and the illiterate. If the collections were combined, they would tell the complete story of Virginia's history. "VHS would house a tremendously rich and diverse picture of Virginia," Wise pointed out to these Board members.

Given his board's interest, Bryan called Wise back and said, "this might be workable. Can we talk again?" The society had already planned a fund-raising drive; it simply added the proposal to build a new wing. One board member, E. Claiborne Robins, Jr. pledged $7 million—the largest known individual cash gift ever given to a historical society in this country, about the same value as a similar gift of property made in Wisconsin by a member of the Kohler family—that would proactively cover the costs. The trustees voted unanimously in favor of the plan.

In January 1996, Governor Allen announced the new partnership. "By teaming up, the Historical Society and the DHR can better ensure that present and future citizens of our Commonwealth—and the nation—are able to learn the full story of Virginia's tremendous history." Ground was broken for the new wing in November 1996 and construction was completed in early 1998 just days after Governor Allen left office.

With their noses pressed against a long wall of glass, students now watch conservation in progress in the first floor state-of-the-art lab. The Department of Historic Resources has its artifacts stored in museum quality space and the staff and programs are accessible to the public. The expanded exhibit space houses "The Story of Virginia," an award-winning permanent exhibit of Virginia history that draws on the collections of both the Historical Society and DHR and occupies the second floor of the new wing. Researchers have access to a wealth of the state's artifacts in the same location. The idea proved as winning as a grandbaby's first smile.

7. When the polluter is Government

One of the biggest polluters in Virginia is not a hog producer, a shipyard, or a utility. It's government—the same authority that's supposed to protect the environment.

—Ledyard King and Scott Harper
The Virginian-Pilot, 3 July 2000

Federal and state environmental laws in a number of fields have established the general principle that, where practicable, the polluter should pay. This is not only a fair notion, holding people responsible for their actions, it's also an intelligent one. When people pay to clean up their own messes, they have an incentive not to create them in the first place.

And what happens when the responsible party is not a person, or a private citizen, but another branch of government, such as a federal agency or another local or state government? Well then, it should pay. This is its clear obligation and duty. Even so, many practical problems arise when the party responsible for a particular environmental mess is not a particular private interest, but some governmental sovereignty. And if companies and citizens would like to avoid having to pay for clean-up, so would many government officials.

In Virginia, it seemed we had more than our share of periodic conflicts with other units of government. There were two cases in particular, though, that brought home to me the difficulty of holding governments accountable for their role in pollution. One involved a large private company—but one that had done much of its polluting while making things for the government. The other involved a federal prison operating in Virginia. Both cases taught me that holding government responsible is not only difficult—it's important to do.

The first of these cases came to my attention in 1994, when the Attorney General's staff requested a meeting with me. My deputy, Tom Hopkins, joined the meeting, as did Harry Kelso, the new enforcement director of the Department of Environmental Quality. We listened as the attorneys laid out an offer to settle a long-running legal battle that had tied up Virginia, the federal government, and several private companies for years. From the way the attorneys explained it, settlement sounded attractive.

In October of 1989, Avtex, a rayon manufacturer with operations in Front Royal, Virginia, had shut down its plant and, by the following February, filed for bankruptcy. The problem from our perspective was that the firm still owed the state millions of dollars in environmental fines. Since then, Virginia and other creditors had been slugging it out over the only valuable thing it had left: several thousand platinum jets used in the manufacturing process. Because the company's owner also left behind a huge environmental liability, Virginia taxpayers were being soaked for substantial clean-up costs and incurring the obligation for future site maintenance.

The idea of putting such a complex and enervating conflict to bed certainly had its appeal. But as the lawyers talked on about the complexities of the case and the desirability of limiting the damage to the state that might follow extended litigation, I kept waiting for them to tell me who was going to clean up the site and when. And the lawyers, for their part, never seemed to get to that point.

In truth, the case was even more tangled and troublesome, than the lawyers conceded in making their case to "get the thing settled." The federal government declared Avtex a Superfund waste site in 1986. In this case, that meant, under the federal Superfund law, Virginia must pay 10 percent of the initial clean-up expenses, and then potentially 100 percent of ongoing maintenance and monitoring costs—customarily a 30-year obligation to ensure that the clean-up goals are reached. The sums could be astronomical. The abandoned Avtex site sat on 440 acres, half of which was covered by 30-foot lagoons filled with chemical sludge. Miles of underground pipe contained calcified waste—including residual carbon disulfide. The building, twice the size of the Pentagon, was a labyrinth of rusting steel, corroded vats, and asbestos lining. Already 4,500 tons of scrap metal, 2,000 tons of chemicals, 8,000 tons of contaminated soil, 2 million gallons of liquid chemicals and contaminated water, and 5,000 drums of toxic material had been either removed or neutralized...and the surface was barely scratched.

Virginia's share of the clean-up and maintenance bill could have topped $100 million.

One thing the lawyers said caught my interest. Avtex, they said had been a government contractor. For many years the company (under the name American Viscose Corporation) manufactured a rubber synthetic for the war production board during World War II. Later the firm made carbonized rayon used in missiles and rockets for several federal agencies. I knew Superfund operated on the principle of "polluter pays"—that taxpayers foot the bill for the clean-up only when the culprit is unknown or unable to pay. I was beginning to wonder if the federal government could in some way be responsible. "Polluter pays" is an important concept that I did not feel we should surrender. No one could answer my questions. *Someone knows who the responsible parties are here*, I thought; and until one of those people was me, I wasn't signing off on any deals.

"Wait a minute," I said to the AG's lawyers. "Virginia is not a polluter here, so why are we on the hook for clean-up costs?"

The attorney general's staff didn't have a good answer for me, and I wanted to find out what was going on.

After the meeting, I asked Kelso to step into my office. "What do you think of this?" I asked him, restating my own concern. "What kind of liability are we exposing Virginia taxpayers to?"

Kelso agreed that something was amiss in the case as it was presented. What he reported back was interesting indeed.

"There is a provision in Superfund by which the Commonwealth can get all its money back," he told me, "and most likely insulate itself from ever getting dinged again in the future." It would require smoking out the responsible parties, and that could be time-consuming. But Kelso had been trained in the Justice Department as Counsel to the Assistant U.S. Attorney General for the Environment and Natural Resources Division, and had served as an environmental enforcement and defense litigator. There he had learned how to turn over every rock hunting for information and evidence. Remembering I had asked for his advice, Kelso gave it to me straight.

"Secretary Dunlop, we ought to think very seriously about suing to recover all our clean-up costs," he advised, "and to put ourselves in a position where we're [Virginians are] not going to be stuck with 10 percent of the costs and potentially 30 years of clean-up operations and maintenance."

"All right," I said. "Let's poke around and see what we find." Mindful it could be a dry hole, I added, "And if we find nothing, then we'll close the door."

Reading Avtex case law, Kelso learned that FMC Corporation—the Chicago-based chemical company and defense contractor that owned the production facility from 1963 to 1976—had sued the federal government to help share the costs. The feds had settled the case, agreeing to reimburse FMC for 35 percent of its clean-up costs. Kelso knew that meant FMC had evidence the feds were somehow culpable. So he papered official Washington with Freedom of Information Act requests, which he filed with the Departments of Justice, Commerce, and Defense, the National Archives, the Navy, the Army, and—a source no one else had thought of—the Reagan Library.

Kelso also learned that FMC had sued its insurance carriers to recover the losses it sustained in clean-up costs and knew the company could be reimbursed only if the damage was deemed sudden and accidental. Kelso checked the verdict; FMC's insurers had not been ordered to pay. That meant the insurers had been able to show FMC was also complicit, Kelso calculated. So FMC was a liable party, and FMC must have had the goods on the feds meaning some part of the federal government was a responsible party also.

"If I can build a paper trail," Kelso told me, briefing me on his progress, "then I can checkmate the feds and FMC and force them to pay Virginia back and insulate us from gargantuan liability if things go wrong [at the site]." I gave him my full support.

For the next few months Kelso worked diligently, quietly fitting together the pieces. Eventually he found a smoking gun. It was a series of memoranda written by the Air Force, buried in the closed-case files Kelso had obtained from the Justice Department. Shuffling through them, incredulous at what he was reading, Kelso knew the case was won. It would take another year to make the facts presentable, but ultimately, Virginia would prevail.

Documents in hand, Kelso walked over to show me the winning ticket. In my outer office, he found Deputy Secretary Tom Hopkins waiting. I was on the phone. Kelso showed him the memoranda and Hopkins, an experienced environmental lawyer himself, understood its implications instantly.

The Defense Department, the Air Force, the Commerce Department and particularly NASA all were culpable in the Avtex mess. They had helped sponsor this environmental liability, and—which I found both disappointing and shocking—*they had known what they were doing when they did it and declined to accept responsibility and help pay for clean-up of the site.*

Hopkins finished reading and looked up, wide-eyed. I was off the phone. "Let's go talk to her," Hopkins said, and listened as Kelso told me this amazing tale that he had pieced together from the documents he had uncovered.

Since its opening in 1940, Avtex was an economic linchpin of Front Royal, Virginia, a small community 90 miles west of Washington, D.C. At its peak, the manufacturing plant employed 3,000 people. But on October 31, 1988, John Gregg, who had bought the company from FMC and renamed the facility "Avtex Fibers Corporation," announced the plant would close on November 18. Gregg said he no longer could afford the dual drains of international competition and environmental regulation.

NASA officials went into orbit when they heard the news, because Avtex was the sole supplier of the rayon used in the space shuttle. If the plant closed, they would have to shut down the program for two years—at a cost of $485 million—until a new supplier could be cultivated.

Immediately, government officials discussed with Avtex what it would take to keep the plant afloat. Auditors estimated that $38 million was required to re-start operations. In addition, they recommended another $5 million for a contingency fund. NASA said it would advance the company $18 million immediately if the Department of Defense would agree to pay the remaining $20 million.

On November 7, 1988, Roger Dekok of the National Security Council (NSC) sent a memo to National Security Advisor Colin Powell, advising him of the situation. Internal National Security Council documents record that "NASA and DOD are still evaluating the effect of last week's closure of the AVTEX Fiber Inc. plant," Dekok wrote. "AVTEX was the single manufacturer of a rayon fiber that is in rocket nozzles and other parts of the space shuttle and missiles. NASA's preliminary reading is that their supply of the product will run out in May 1989."

The National Security Council approved the bailout.

Two days later, NASA advanced Avtex $7 million to fund its short-term operation, along with $70,000 to meet payroll. The government was pushing a rayon production in a plant it knew to be a serious environmental problem for the Commonwealth of Virginia.

On November 29, 1988, there was a staff-level meeting of the NSC in the Old Executive Office Building on the White House grounds. A broad host of agencies were represented, including the Air Force, the Defense Department, NASA, the State Department, the Departments of Commerce, Transportation, and Justice, the Office of Management and Budget, the Federal Emergency Management Agency and the Environmental Protection Agency.

Jim Miskel of Powell's staff opened the meeting by asking for an update on the situation. George Abbey from NASA reported that the factory was about two days away from re-opening and expected to be fully operational again by mid-December. Steve Wassersug of the EPA described the environmental programs affecting Avtex and handed out a matrix showing probable costs for clean-up. He said the EPA was modeling the carbon disulfide emissions, which could prove to be an imminent and substantial danger to the public health and the environment.

"Will any of the money that has gone to Avtex be used to finance clean-up?" asked John Richards of Commerce.

"No," Wassersug told him.

Marcia Mulkey of the EPA said notice letters would be sent out the next week to parties considered potentially responsible for the environmental liability at Avtex. That raised some interesting issues regarding liability, she warned. Because NASA was an investor into Avtex, Mulkey explained, the federal government could be considered a responsible party. Wassersug asked both NASA and the Defense Department to have a chat with their legal staffs. But neither he nor anyone else from EPA is known to have objected to the federal government subsidizing what it knew was a huge environmental liability. Meanwhile, Virginia continued pursuing litigation against Avtex for violating environmental laws, which the company, flush with cash from the feds, blithely refused to obey. In August, 1989, Governor Gerald Baliles wrote to EPA Administrator William Reilly relating the events and the state's persistent problems with the plant. Baliles said he was "appalled" to learn how poorly the EPA had responded to chronic problems and asked that the agency institute an enforcement action against Avtex and clean up the facility. Finally, on November 9, 1989—citing more than 2,000 pollution violations—the state's Water Control Board decided to revoke one of Avtex's operating permits, effectively shutting down the Front Royal plant.

"You cannot close the plant overnight," Gregg warned Virginia Deputy Attorney General Claire Guthrie. "It is going to be an ecological disaster for someone to try to clean up after viscose [material] sets [in the system]. The other problem obviously is that we have on hand a substantial inventory of heavy chemicals, acids, caustics plus CS2." Once power was shut off, he explained, "we no longer have the ability to do the work necessary to clean these liquids from the Front Royal site." Gregg asked Guthrie for more time. "[I have] instructed our people to shut this plant down unless we get an extension," he told her, "and it essentially means a 'walk-away' because we will not have the ability to do anything in terms of cleaning up."

Guthrie refused to grant his request, and Gregg fired back a petulant response. "The Plant will be down between 5 and 6 p.m. today, November 10, so we will be in compliance with your Order." That evening he closed the doors and left the mess to the care of the Commonwealth.

Because the plant represented an environmental "emergency," Virginia taxpayers and EPA immediately began pouring millions into trying to clean up the mess, while the two principally responsible parties, Avtex Fibers and the U.S. space agency, contributed nothing.

When FMC sued the government in 1991 to make it pay its share, though, government lawyers recognized a problem. Major Richard Sarver of the Air Force's environmental litigation branch assessed the pros and cons of reaching a settlement.

> The clearest reason to accept this offer [is financial prudence]. There is also a potential for adverse publicity attending either a victory or loss on the liability issue....The

theme of any such publicity will be the United States bailing out an environmentally unsound company and walking away from the mess after getting what it wanted.

EPA will testify that the Avtex site was 'an abomination' and one of the worst sites ever observed by a very experienced on-site coordinator, Sarver continued. The Virginia witnesses will testify that Avtex was the worst polluter in Virginia during its last year of operations and that this information was conveyed to DOD and NASA. Avtex employees will testify that the plant could not have been reopened but for the infusion of cash from NASA and DOD.

All things considered, Sarver concluded, NASA and DOD benefited greatly from the reopening of the Avtex plant. "Perhaps it is right that we contribute to the clean-up."

Its hand forced, the government had reimbursed FMC thirty-five cents on the dollar. But left Virginia holding the bag.

Kelso had uncovered the answers I was seeking, and now he offered advice. "The people of this state should not have to pay a dime for the catastrophic environmental mess that the United States government caused," Kelso said. I agreed.

At this point, having ascertained the facts, we met with the Governor. Surprising neither of us, Governor Allen agreed that, far from dropping the case, we should press the federal government to correct the injustice. If it did not, Virginia would take the United States to court. I directed Kelso to press ahead.

The first order of business was to brief Virginia's congressional delegation that the state was about to take on the feds. "I am second to none in supporting the military," Kelso told them. "But we can't have the state left holding the bag for a catastrophe the military and NASA knowingly caused and the EPA ignored." Virginia's congressmen agreed.

In September, 1996, Kelso began negotiations with the Justice Department's Environment and Natural Resources

Division. After a second meeting at the end of December, Justice halted discussion. Though they had to understand Kelso had the goods, the government's lawyers decided to ignore him.

So on February 19, 1997, Tom Hopkins, now the Director of DEQ, sent a letter to Attorney General Janet Reno. On behalf of the Commonwealth, he insisted that the federal government should reimburse Virginia for what the state had spent so far on clean-up, pick up its share of future costs, and assume responsibility for any problems the site might cause in the future. Additionally, the Allen Administration wanted the government to pay a civil penalty of nearly $500 million. The feds either could pony up voluntarily, Hopkins said, or face a lawsuit in which the courts would order payment. Their "deliberate concealment" had yielded a situation "nothing short of cataclysmic," he wrote—cataclysmic, of course, for their credibility.

Hopkins was not coy with Reno. He made it clear he had her dead to rights, quoting the excruciatingly incriminating Air Force memos.

To be specific, Hopkins wrote, the chief environmental lawyer for the U.S. Air Force, in a 1991 memo, stated in part:

> First, there is evidence that [the Department of Defense] and NASA did not act responsibly toward the environmental problems at Avtex. There is evidence that DOD and NASA knew of the huge environmental problem facing Avtex and did not take any action to ensure that these problems were solved. There is also evidence that DOD and NASA pushed Avtex for as much production as possible, all the while knowing that an environmental disaster was brewing....There is evidence that the last year of operation added disproportionately to the cost of clean-up of the site. There are other problems with our case, but the reason for considering these elements in evaluating this settlement is that during the allocation phase of trial the so-called "Gore factors" will be used to determine the shares of liability. Under those factors our share of liability may increase because of what may be perceived as irresponsible conduct in connection with Avtex's last year of operation.

"Other official U.S. documents not only confirm this posture," Hopkins went on, "but amplify on the contractual relationship" between the government and Avtex. Hopkins cited another incriminating memo, which read in part: "Evidence shows that NASA-DOD knew of environmental problems at site and did little or nothing to remedy them; that NASA-DOD pumped money into facility to revive it, and pushed it to produce rayon." The relationships between the government and Avtex, one of the government's own analysts admitted, "were arguably joint venturers." Those federal agencies, in fact, "had the power to make Avtex comply with environmental standards but failed to exercise it." In fact, U.S. officials had "pressured suppliers of Avtex to supply the facility with products which contributed to contamination."

Announcing publicly that Virginia was seeking a settlement from the feds, Allen summarized the situation. "Federal agencies were in a joint venture with the companies operating the rayon factory, knowing full well that by doing so the United States government was condoning an environmental catastrophe in the making," he said. "These operations have polluted our groundwater, contaminated the land, and generally denigrated the environment—and now Virginians are being expected to help pay for its clean-up. That's not right or fair."

Perhaps not wanting to make any concessions in a Virginia election year, and perhaps out of mere stubbornness, Reno refused to budge. Within days, we filed suit in U.S. District Court against the Defense Department, The Air Force and NASA, as well as FMC, claiming the government knew the site was a "serious environment danger, but did nothing about it, citing national security precautions."

In June 1997, Virginia's Deputy Attorney General John Paul Woodley and Assistant Attorney General Stewart Leeth recommended that I accept a settlement offer they had negotiated. "Specifically, the government defendants would collectively pay

35 percent of Virginia's past and future costs at the Avtex site," wrote Leeth. "I have reviewed the offer and the applicable law and recommend the settlement."

I turned it down. Though the attorney general's office kept encouraging us to take these offers, I thought we should keep pressing. First, we represented the people of Virginia, and it was our duty to get them the best deal possible. This was particularly true as the Superfund law generally holds each responsible party liable for 100 percent of all clean-up costs.

Second, and equally important, it was fair, and it was good policy to make the federal government meet its responsibilities. If we didn't, I felt, we would just be encouraging more such cases in the future—more pollution, more bailouts, and more secret deals to keep a polluting plant in operation but stiff the states with the bill.

One month later, the lawyers tried to get me to accept another settlement offer. "EPA will reimburse Virginia for the balance of any past costs not recovered by Virginia from the United States Defendants and from FMC under the proposed settlement," they informed me. Moreover, this offer was accompanied by threats. The EPA's lawyer advised further that Virginia's failure to cooperate with EPA would be "viewed by EPA as a breach," Leeth wrote, of the mutual cooperation covenants found in the State Superfund Contract. If Virginia refused its offer, the agency's lawyer continued, he would recommend that "the Avtex site would remain a Superfund site well into the future."

"In light of these developments," wrote Leeth, "I recommend that Virginia accept the offers made by the defendants and by EPA *as to past costs only* and reserve our right to pursue any and all of the defendants for Virginia's future costs, if any."

The timidity of our own attorney general's staff stunned me. These attorneys were working for Virginia? I notified them that this offer, too, was unacceptable. I was insistent that "*the entire bill* for cleaning up this site and restoring it should be paid by those who caused the problem to occur and/or continue without regard to the people of the Commonwealth."

134

I also briefed Governor Allen on the pattern of negotiations between the federal government and my office and the attorney general's. I did not want to proceed without the Governor having the chance to be made familiar with the issues and make his own decision. Perhaps the Governor would feel, with the attorney general's staff, that we should settle the suit.

After reviewing the issues with perspective from all the relevant offices, the Governor decided as I had expected he would—we would only accept a settlement offer in which the federal government agreed to pay the its full contribution to the site clean-up.

If the tables were turned, and Virginia or some private enterprise had the liability, the Governor asked during one conversation, what would the EPA do?

"They would make us pay," I answered. "There wouldn't even be the kind of discussion we're having."

With the Governor standing firm, the feds finally blinked. By October, there was a settlement. Virginia taxpayers would be reimbursed for what they had already spent cleaning up the Avtex site, and the EPA would allocate $33 million to demolish the building remaining. Kelso wanted one more thing: the feds to pay attorney's fees. He demanded they reimburse Virginia for what it had paid the bankruptcy attorney as well as the $10,000 it cost to put the case together. The feds paid.

"We brought this lawsuit to hold accountable those who were responsible for this environmental disaster," announced a satisfied Allen, "and we succeeded." Watching George Allen make that announcement, I was proud of him in a double sense. First, he had just plain hung tough, when the attorney general's office wanted to throw in the towel. Secondly, he had brought in significant funding to help Virginia's environment—and he was punishing the violators.

On November 11, 1997, at 9:50 a.m., the Avtex Fibers plant became history. Eighty pounds of dynamite transformed its 30-story smokestacks into a pile of brick rubble. Completing the clean-up will cost millions but now that the FMC Corporation has major responsibility for the remediation, Front Royal can expect parcels of this site to be restored to economic and community uses in just a few years. And, monitoring will continue for sometime into this century, but that will be the federal government's financial responsibility, not that of Virginia taxpayers.

Thanks to Governor Allen's willingness to demonstrate the importance of the "polluter pays" principle in environmental law, combined with Harry Kelso's masterful detective work, the state's taxpayers were spared from shelling out $100 million into a bottomless bank account with no responsible party and a perpetual Superfund lawyer's goldmine was put on the path of real remediation.

Lorton federal prison in southeastern Fairfax County was a boil on Virginia's backside. When it was built in 1916 to house prisoners for the District of Columbia, it was surrounded by miles and miles of farms. By the summer of 1996, Lorton held more than 6,000 inmates in the state's most populous county. Worse: District officials were utterly inept at maintaining the facility properly. Inmates escaped—once, seven at a time—operated drug rings inside the prison, and, peeved by the inherent limitations of confinement, had even set fire to the place.

But of greatest detriment to most Virginians was the delight the prisoners took in playing a game called "cretins." Simply put, cretins meant trying to flush unflushable items down the toilets, causing sewage-line breaks, overflows, and horrible smells not only throughout the prison, but for miles around the jail.

Lorton's inadequate sewage system had been a problem for nearly a decade. Although the District had agreed to upgrade the prison's treatment plant, and had done so repeatedly, the problem was getting worse. Since August of 1995, separate overflows of the Lorton sewage system had dumped more than 2 million gallons into nearby creeks. The worst such episode was in April, 1996, when more than 2 million gallons of raw sewage overflowed from a prison manhole into Mills Branch, a feeder into the Occoquan River where Virginians boat, fish, and swim. A DEQ employee photographed the creek—teeming with toilet paper and other debris.

It was especially maddening that the EPA Regional Director and Earth Day maestro Mike McCabe, who was now responsible for overseeing D.C. water pollution performance, had time to antagonize Virginia about DEQ reorganization, undertake the overfiling of the Virginia Smithfield enforcement case, and micromanage other matters, but couldn't keep his own outhouse in order. Had Virginia been dumping raw sewage, especially in an election year, who would doubt that the EPA would be in hot pursuit? Why shouldn't the federal EPA be just as tough on the only prison for which it was responsible?

I wanted the District fined substantially, given its continuous violations even after repeated warnings and consent orders. I generally took a dim view of fines in the case of local governments, but thought differently when the federal government was involved—as it is in the case of almost any policy or dispute involving the District of Columbia, where final authority is an amalgam of home rule and federal oversight.

"The federal government is the nation's biggest polluter," I pointed out. "Do you really want to let the biggest polluter in the country get away with virtually no fine after the almost continuous violations of their consent order?" Even in baseball, you are out after three strikes. The Allen Administration had been faced with a persistent whine from EPA that our "compliance first" actions, as compared to the "fine 'em" first approach favored by EPA, was evidence of our supposed lack of commitment to protecting the environment. In this situation, we had worked to get the prison into compliance and it just was not working. A stiff fine was appropriate and deserved.

The lawyers from the AG's office weren't moved by any of my efforts at collegial, personal persuasion to get the federal government's attention on this serious Lorton problem. Deputy DEQ Director March Bell explained that we intended to take the matter public and it was up to the Attorney General's office to demand a reasonable fine from the District of Columbia. Bell advised that the Secretary would hold a press conference and announce she wanted a new consent order and a fine of $175,000, an amount commensurate with the continued violations. Then the lawyers could explain their position.

So the Attorney General publicly put Washington, D.C., on notice. Dumping sewage into Virginia's waters was "not something I can put up with," he said. "Enough is enough," Gilmore announced at a September 18, 1996 press conference. If his concerns were not addressed within the next 10 days, the Commonwealth would sue.

"These discharges threaten the water quality of Virginia waters, including Mills Branch, Giles Run, the Occoquan River, Belmont Bay, and Occoquan Bay," Gilmore said. "The Potomac River and the Chesapeake Bay are the ultimate targets of this pollution. I intend to do all in my power to protect these resources."

Questioned point-blank about his motives, Gilmore responded with vigorous righteous indignation. "I am not going to stand for the idea that because we are concerned for the public health, that is political," he declared. "I would hope [D.C. officials] would take this matter seriously. I consider it very serious."

I was glad Gilmore was on board. It was the right thing to do. And, having decided against the apparent counsel of the staff attorneys on his payroll, he was smart to do it aggressively and in public. Tom Hopkins represented the DEQ at the press conference making brief remarks in support of the Attorney General's action.

It always seemed to me that the career attorneys at the Attorney General's office preferred to negotiate settlements rather than litigate or take bold action again consistent violators.

Gilmore's announcement also meant our Administration was united in front of the press and in negotiating with D.C. and Administrator McCabe. The ultimate beneficiaries were the people up in Fairfax County who had lived with the Lorton pollution for so long a time.

Four months later, an agreement was reached. The District would pay a $25,000 fine and apply the balance of the $175,000 toward solving the problem and, most importantly, would now abide by all Virginia's environmental regulations, as well as correct the deplorable situation at Lorton.

Lorton would complete all repairs to the treatment facility within the next 18 months, by June 1998.

In addition, Virginia's DEQ could inspect the prison's sewage treatment facility at any time.

The feds would have expected as much of Virginia. I expected no less from them.

A sequel was reported in February 2000. The State Water Control Board filed a court motion to fine the District of Columbia at least $175,000 for alleged sewage violations at the District's prison in Lorton, according to the Associated Press. The District has violated a judge's orders by failing to fix the sewage system, according to Attorney General Mark Earley's office. And, EPA is still "missing in action" from this battlefield, the only one for which it has direct responsibility and authority.

8. The cost and hypocrisy of 0.00000004 less smog

November 27, 1996—it was the day before Thanksgiving; one of the few days in the year when Americans are completely unified in purpose.

Did you remember to pick up the cranberry sauce? Who is picking up Aunt Cora? Come on, get these toys off the living room floor. Have you forgotten company is coming?

For the next four days, the nation's attention would be collectively riveted on parades and footballs and family and food.

It was the perfect time for the EPA to announce onerous new regulations that would cost Americans billions of dollars and produce no measurable gain.

By releasing the information on Wednesday, the EPA ensured that reports about the proposed standards would appear in newspapers on Thanksgiving Day, editions likely to be read by only a few bored police officers, waitresses, and emergency-room workers.

Lamentably, many Americans would miss the news of the EPA's latest antics, which was this: If the agency had its way, by summer the legal limit for ozone concentration, or smog, would drop from .12 parts per million to .08 parts per million measured over eight hours, and there would be new standards for particulate matter. EPA would change the form of the current 24-hour PM 10 standard and add new standards for particulates smaller than 2.5 micrometers in diameter (PM 2.5).

To put those figures in context, an ozone concentration of .08 parts per million is only slightly higher than the level of ozone produced by natural vegetation. A level of .072 ppm has been recorded in North Dakota's Theodore Roosevelt National Park, about as remote a place as one can find in North America. As for the 2.5 micron particulate-matter limit: a 2.5 micron airborne particulate of dust is roughly thirty times smaller than the width of a human hair.

"The EPA proposal would provide new protection to nearly 133 million Americans, including 40 million children," claimed Browner. But not only did she offer no data to support that claim, much of the agency's research directly contradicted it. In EPA experiments, subjects exposed to the lower ozone levels had not shown appreciably different lung function than under current conditions. As for children, the EPA's best-case scenario projected that lowered standards would help only about half of those with impaired lung function.

Browner acknowledged that "many, including some Democrats in Congress, disagreed with the new standards" and conceded the opposition's reasoning. By any measure, the Clean Air Act had already been a success. Since its passage a quarter century ago, the country's population has risen by 28 percent and the economy has nearly doubled. Yet emissions of the six major pollutants or their precursors have actually dropped by 29 percent. Why, then, many were asking, did the federal government propose to move the goal posts?

It was a good question for which Browner offered a boldly disingenuous answer. "Science now tells us that our air pollution standards are not adequate to protect the public's health," she said. "The best, current, peer-reviewed, fully debated scientific conclusions are that too many Americans are not being protected by the current standards." At a Senate hearing, she waved a bibliography of some 271 studies—we would have loved to have seen that document, but did not—purporting to show that "hospitalization" and "deaths" were resulting from pollution levels that were still too high.

The only science that was available for true scientific review, though—which is the only real science there is—hardly justified Browner's rhetoric. Unable to reach any firm conclusions, the EPA's advisors the Clean Air Scientific Advisory Committee, had recommended the agency make an administrative decision. "The diversity of opinion expressed by the panel members reflected the many unanswered questions and large uncertainties," said the head of the advisory panel, George Wolff. As for the "best science" they had reviewed: Of the 185 ozone-related studies to which Browner referred, only 31 tested the health effects of ozone exposure alone. Most examined other factors, such things as sex-based reaction differences.

Only eight of the EPA studies actually were relevant, i.e., experimented with ozone levels at current and proposed standards. The studies reached different conclusions—one finding, for instance, that though more people tend to die on days with high pollution levels, the correlation disappears when humidity is factored in.

EPA also ignored what Ronald Reagan was once scorned for pointing out—that volatile organic compounds occur naturally as trees and other vegetation produce oxygen and hydrocarbons. A 1991 study by the prestigious National Academy of Sciences found that in Atlanta and other parts of the Southeast, vegetation produced more such chemicals than cars or factories.

Most critically, Browner was ignoring the Center for Disease Control, which had concluded after a 1996 study of asthma-related deaths that "no evidence exists that supports the role of outdoor pollution levels as the primary factor driving the changes in the epidemiological patterns of asthma morbidity."

Perhaps anticipating that many would question the astounding dismissal of data, Browner later said, "The question is not one of science. The question is one of judgment." This was a much more accurate statement. And her judgment was that not only scientists, but also economists should be ignored. When Browner claimed the new restrictions would cost no more than $8.5 billion annually, Alicia Munnell of the President Clinton's Council of Economic Advisers demurred. The EPA "understates the true costs of stricter standards by orders of magnitude," said

Munnell. "CEA estimates indicate that the cost of full attainment could be up to $60 billion."

The EPA even went so far as to manipulate a critical report from the Office of Management and Budget, the agency required by law to analyze new rulings and determine whether they make sense. Like almost everyone else, the OMB concluded the new air-quality standards did not. The Office of Science and Technology had reported the line between soot and illness "cannot be established." Assistant Transportation Secretary Frank Kruesi told a budget office official "it appears incomprehensible that the administration would commit to a new set of standards...without a much greater understanding of the problem and its solutions."

But rather than report that conclusion directly to Congress, the OMB let the fox into the henhouse. When Tom Bliley asked the budget office whether the EPA had complied with federal guidelines in drafting the new rules, he received an answer that sounded as if it had been written by the EPA itself—and probably was. Internal memos indicate the EPA was unhappy with the budget office's unfavorable findings, so proposed rewriting the report "line by line." Browner's deputy, John Beale, wrote that the budget office letter to Bliley must be reworded because "as written, the response could be very damaging."

More worrisome for the EPA: The public was beginning to understand that the standards could bring additional government restrictions, such as when (or if) they could mow their lawns or cook burgers on the grill.

Browner accused her critics of playing fast and loose with the truth, a most brazen assertion. "I am disappointed that some have chosen to distort this important discussion by raising distracting and misleading pseudo-issues like 'banning backyard barbecues'," she told a Senate panel. But as Browner spoke, the EPA was pushing restrictions on lawn mowers, leaf blowers, fireplaces, lighter fluid, and motorboats. In March, the second phase of lawn- and garden-equipment regulations had been announced. Denver already had outlawed fireplaces in new homes, trying to placate the feds. Residents of Albuquerque faced 90 days in jail if they burned wood on days it was forbidden. If the EPA wasn't targeting backyard barbecues, certainly that day was coming. As the Clinton Transportation Department put it, "Control measures needed to meet the standards could...require lifestyle changes by a significant part of the U.S. population."

The problem Browner faced in trying to justify the stricter standards was that the clean-air battle essentially had been won. Industry and car emissions had been so sanitized that they no longer were primary pollutants. In Baltimore, for instance—which competed with Washington as the city with the dirtiest air on the East Coast—motorboats and lawn mowers contributed more to the city's smog problem than all the city's industry combined. That was not testament to Baltimore's filthy boats and grass clippers, but to the pristine quality of air required by the nation's stringent standards.

The rules were so strict that some experts estimated that if all cars were banned from Los Angeles and Washington, D.C., those cities *still* could not meet the EPA's new rules.

Faced with a gathering storm, Browner did what, in my experience, she nearly always did: She escalated her threats and rhetoric. She told a Senate panel that "scientists already know more about the ill effects of particulates than they knew about the dangers of lead when leaded gasoline was banned decades ago."

Former EPA assistant administrator Robert Sansom read the quotation in *The Washington Post.* Early in the 1970's, Sansom had made the first recommendation to reduce lead in gasoline, and he took issue with Browner's claim, writing the paper:

> I have seen much of EPA's documentation for its proposed more stringent fine particulate and ozone standards. What I have seen I find deficient in many respects...It is a gross exaggeration to compare this EPA proposal to the removal of lead from gasoline. It is nothing more than an effort by Ms. Browner to gain creditability by association rather than on the basis of scientific evidence.

The scientists who advised the EPA on the new standards essentially conceded as much to Congress, testifying that the agency made a "policy judgment" about regulations, not a scientific decision. "Right now, we are a bit in the dark," panelist Morton Lippmann told lawmakers.

Many Congressmen thought Browner was being dishonest and unreasonable. Not surprisingly, Republicans were denouncing the new standards as "regulatory fraud." Congressman Bob Barr suggested Browner recuse herself from discussions because she was clearly unwilling to be objective, pointing to a speech she had made in which she vowed she "would not be swayed" by data.

But even leading Democrats asked her to reconsider the new rules. Senators Robert Byrd, John Glenn, Wendell Ford, Chuck Robb, and John Rockefeller wrote her in March to express their concern. "Because of the significant uncertainty surrounding the costs, benefits, and impacts of EPA's proposed ozone and [fine particle] rules," the Democrats said, "we urge the EPA to reaffirm the current standards...before embarking on entirely new and costly undertakings."

The most stunning defection came when the late Senator John Chafee, one of the nation's most ardent advocates of environmental law, announced reservations about the new standards. Browner had achieved what many thought impossible: She had pushed Chafee to the limit. "These are very complex and far-reaching proposals," he said at a Senate hearing. "After careful review, I am concerned that they may be too far-reaching. It is possible to push too far, too fast." Coming from Chafee, that was akin to the proverbial man-bites-dog story.

Perhaps hoping to appease critics, the EPA did reduce to 15,000 the fictitious number of Americans it said died every year because of pollution. Using the EPA's own statistical model, a pair of private analysts calculated that figure at 840. "In fact the risk is likely lower. No biologically plausible mechanism exists to explain how particulate matter, at current concentrations, contributes to mortality," Kay Jones and Michael Gough wrote in

The Detroit News. "It is conceivable that the risk is zero at current exposures."

In ordinary circumstances—in real-world science—independent researchers simply would have replicated the original studies. If the results were the same, that would validate the initial findings. But this was EPA science. Joel Schwartz, the EPA contract scientist whose work was the basis for the revised standards, refused to share his data. He characterized public scrutiny of his work as harassment and denounced as "industry thugs" scientists asking to duplicate his findings. Schwartz refused "to have to spend endless time arguing about a continuing series of industry re-analyses."

Even Mary Nichols, an assistant administrator under Browner, had little patience with Schwartz's argument. "When lots of money and lives are at stake," Nichols said, "it's not appropriate to say, 'This is my data and nobody should be looking at it.'" But Schwartz would not budge, even as his declarations grew more hostile.

Bliley sent a letter to Browner pointing out that the agency had the right to get "the underlying data and supplementary materials for the studies"—for which it had paid—and that she should exercise her authority to request the data. His letter was answered by Nichols, but the verbiage in my judgment was vintage Browner.

"We do not believe...there is a useful purpose for EPA to obtain the underlying data....

"Securing more detail about this information is not necessary as part of EPA's public health standard-setting process."

Nichols, though, always the loyal lieutenant, soon had the mantra down pat. Testifying on the new standards to a House subcommittee, she recited: "Over the past three and a half years, EPA has conducted one of its most thorough and extensive scientific reviews ever. That review is the basis for the new, more stringent standards for particulate matter and ozone that we have proposed in order to fulfill the mandate of the Clean Air Act."

Very few were buying it. One of the leading opponents of the new standards was Congressman John Dingell, a senior Democrat who helped rewrite the Clean Air Act in 1990. "I support the Clean Air Act," said Dingell. "I support the regulations now in place." The new rules, he argued, would "impose enormous economic burdens on American business," he commented, while conferring "doubtful health benefits." The agency, he added, was "making an emotional appeal" and was "not using good analytical work" to back it up.

"EPA," the senior Democrat concluded, "has not played with a fair deck."

In April 1997, Dingell, along with 41 other Democrats, wrote the President and criticized the proposed regulation. At an agency oversight hearing in May, Dingell took on Browner. Business leaders had unified to oppose the standards *en masse*. Led by Detroit Mayor Dennis Archer, a staunch Clinton-Gore supporter, the U.S. Conference of Mayors passed a resolution opposing the new standards. In Congress, legislation to postpone the new rules was rapidly gaining supporters and looked strong enough potentially to override a presidential veto. State legislatures began passing resolutions opposing the tightened standards. But nowhere was the debate fiercer than inside the walls of the White House.

President Clinton's advisers had explained to him that the new standards were scientifically indefensible and would be economically disastrous; he was reluctant to support them. On the other hand, Clinton did not want to cost Gore the support of environmental radicals. Clinton, naturally, wanted to have it both ways in the form of new, but much diluted, standards. Browner was not having any of that; she had drawn a line in the sand. Not science nor reason nor her boss's wishes had any impact on her.

148

The president was angry that Browner had boxed him in publicly. "He likes a good healthy debate," one adviser said, "but he likes it to be kept at the table." Browner's stubbornness also was causing trouble for Gore. With the 2000 election looming, Gore hardly could afford to lose the support of nearly everyone but a handful of extremists. His public silence about the new standards had not gone unnoticed by the radicals on the left, or by Democrats in the congressional center.

"Since this is a top priority issue for the national environmental community at this time," said Gene Karpinksi of the U.S. Public Interest Research Groups in a barely veiled threat, "any weakening of public health protection by the White House would certainly be a huge negative for Vice President Gore that would not be forgotten."

Though sources described Clinton as being "distressed" by the severe economic losses he had been assured by Treasury Secretary Bob Rubin were inevitable, he ultimately decided that needlessly burdening 250 million Americans was a fair price to pay to protect Gore's career. Browner knew Gore had won over Clinton, and she couldn't help gloating about that. The Vice President had added "the right push at the right time," she boasted, to gain Clinton's support for the new standards. An editorial in *The Washington Times* urged readers tongue in cheek to give Browner her due.

> It was Mrs. Browner, after all, who carefully ignored the findings of the agency's own Science Advisory Board, which challenged the notion that the proposed ozone standard would be any more protective of human health than the current one. It was Mrs. Browner who couldn't be bothered to release the data underlying the rule, her public protests notwithstanding, for inspection by more impartial experts. It was Mrs. Browner who brushed aside the concerns of mayors, minority groups, scientists, and a bipartisan group of lawmakers to ram through the rule. And it was Mrs. Browner who backed the administration into a very public corner from which there was no way out by the announcement of the

President's endorsement. If you like the way this White
House operates, wait until Mr. Gore takes charge.

Gore and Browner were essentially alone, pummeled by
bipartisan opposition. But Gore had long made clear his
willingness to foist change on an unwilling citizenry. "It is
essential that we refuse to wait for the obvious signs of impending
catastrophe," he had said. "There are terrible moral consequences
to the current policy of delay, just as there were when we tried to
postpone World War II. Then, as now, the real enemy was a
dysfunctional way of thinking." That dysfunctional thinking
manifested itself, he believed, in a recalcitrant public.

In the end, as in many other policies, the outcome may
have satisfied a few hard core supporters, but at the cost of
alienating many—and without a policy victory. Members of
Congress threatened a congressional review and an overturn of the
regulations, while private interests filed a lawsuit against them.
Some years later, it is still possible the regulations will never be
implemented—although in a Gore presidency it seems there would
almost certainly be an effort to revive the proposal.

Tuesday, July 15, 1997—It was summertime in Virginia,
and the living wasn't easy. A high-pressure system stagnated over
the Mid-Atlantic States; Virginia, Maryland, and Washington,
D.C., were sweltering. The nation's capital was a particular
problem. Monday's high had been 97 degrees. Highs were in the
upper nineties on Tuesday as well, and forecast to remain there for
several days. Combined with high ozone levels, the weather
pushed Washington's air-quality index to 156 on July 15th—on a
scale ranking 100 as "unhealthful." In Baltimore, the index reached
180. Stuart Freudberg of the District of Columbia's Department of
Environmental Programs said he was "pretty sure it's the highest
rating we've had in the last five years." But no one knew for sure

how bad the problem was because the plane used by the University of Maryland to measure ozone levels was grounded—due to poor visibility.

City residents without access to air conditioning were welcomed at various "cooling centers" around town. At the YMCA's 30 summer camps in Washington, outdoor play was canceled. After one director tried to insist the youngsters in his program play outside, counselors brought the children back in, reporting breathing difficulties. Record-breaking amounts of electricity were being consumed, according to Potomac Electric Power Company. At noon, 64-year-old Mary Corsey was found dead in bed by her son. In her top-floor apartment, with the windows shut, she had succumbed to the heat.

Local governments and conscientious citizens were trying to cope with the conditions. Washington's Department of Public Works sent its employees home at noon for the second straight day. Some lawn-mowing services in the District had given their workers the day off, too. Officials had issued a Code Red ozone alert, asking everyone to avoid idling their car engines, refueling before dusk, or operating unnecessary motors such as lawnmowers.

In Virginia, I was doing everything within my power to hold down ozone levels. The state was urging workers to use public transportation. We had canceled road paving and highway mowing until the weather improved. State employees were told not to do any non-essential traveling. But at 3:20 that afternoon, the temperature had registered 98 degrees at Washington's Reagan National Airport, and forecasters were predicting another scorcher—another Code Red alert—which meant more ozone exceedances were likely—for Wednesday.

Three consecutive days in which the ozone level was exceeded in Northern Virginia was not helpful in our efforts to come into compliance with Clean Air rules and could put Virginians subject to more rigorous regulations. Oppressive heat was the gateway to more oppression from the federal government.

I decided that if ozone levels were as unhealthy as the EPA maintained, then certainly it threatened people's health to be out and about in this weather. And didn't the federal government have an obligation not to create conditions for which it penalized states? When snow and ice reached levels considered dangerous, the feds instructed employees to stay home. Why should the dangerous conditions of high ozone levels be treated any differently?

At 6:00 p.m., I faxed a letter to White House Chief of Staff Erskine Bowles, asking that the federal government be shut down on Wednesday, July 16, for the sake of the environment.

"We believe this circumstance requires that the federal government demonstrate its commitment and leadership by closing for the day—as it would in a snow emergency," I wrote, "with only essential personnel reporting to work on Wednesday and for the duration of the 'Code Red' conditions." I urged Bowles to act "in the best interests of the environment and the health of our citizens—our children and others who may be at particular risk."

After allowing a little time to pass and hearing nothing from the White House, I followed up with a phone call, but I only reached Bowles's voice mailbox. Around 9:00 p.m., I called the White House operator, explaining that my question required immediate attention. Shortly thereafter I received a return call from Thurgood Marshall, Jr., newly appointed to his job in the Office of Cabinet Affairs.

The conscientious Marshall told me he would arrange a conference call among his office, the Office of Personnel Management, and the Environmental Protection Agency, and set about rousing people at home to discuss Virginia's request. OPM director Janice Lachance walked the others through the process. She explained, correctly, that there was no government-wide policy for when air quality threatened health. The "Misery Index"—in practice since 1920, when few office buildings were air-conditioned—had set cut-and-dry standards for heat. Workers could be sent home when indoor temperature-to-humidity ratios reached 95 degrees and 55 percent, 96 degrees and 52 percent, 97 degrees and 49 percent, 98 degrees and 45 percent, or 99 degrees and 42 percent. At 100 degrees, no matter what the humidity, employees were relieved from their duties. The guidelines became official in the summer of 1963 as The Civil Service Commission Employee Letter B-193.

But in the summer of 1981, President Reagan replaced that with a new directive: Henceforth, "dismissals due to unusual employment or work conditions created by a temporary disruption of air-cooling or heating systems should be rare....Employees are expected to work if conditions...are reasonably adequate in the agency's judgment, although these conditions may not be normal and may involve minor discomforts."

But the Reagan rule added: "Individual employees affected...to the extent that they are incapacitated for duty, or to the extent that continuance on duty would adversely affect their health, may be granted annual or sick leave."

Though the Reagan Administration was trying to install flexibility and bring the policy up-to-date—in fairness, it hardly was sensible to retain a policy written before air-conditioning was universal—many people preferred concrete standards to ones dependent on a supervisor's discretion.

"I'm not sure you can call it 'progress'," said one, "when the bureaucracy shifts from a simple policy with absolute, written numerical guidelines...to one in which the bottom line is it isn't unbearably hot until the boss says so."

Reagan's policy, moreover, did make an allowance the old one had not: the provision that workers should be sent home when weather conditions endangered their health. So if Browner insisted present ozone levels endangered the lives of half the country's population—and, with those levels exceeded, many more citizens evidently were in jeopardy—then why wouldn't the federal government take seriously such an enormous threat?

Lachance pointed out that giving a day off to federal employees in the Washington area would cost taxpayers $73 million, which was an odd argument, considering environmental extremism holds that the value of a clean environment is too important to be measured in dollars and cents. Indeed, the Clean Air Act expressly forbids the EPA from taking financial considerations into account when setting clean air standards. I admitted the shutdown would be expensive, but "the question is the standard of air quality being unhealthy."

"Look, I used to work there," I reminded the White House staffers. "I know you have until about 6:00 a.m. to make a decision and get it announced on the news. Think about it."

Perhaps they did actually think, but the answer was *no*. Ozone levels were not considered serious enough to warrant such severe action.

Just as the forecasters had predicted, July 16 turned out to be another Code Red day in Washington. With the imprimatur of the White House, nitrogen oxides were billowing into Northern Virginia from typically heavy commuter traffic. I was annoyed, but did not know what more I could have done. The Clinton Administration had implicitly advised me ozone was not a problem real enough to treat seriously.

Meanwhile, in the Roosevelt Room of the White House—not the Rose Garden—a ceremony was beginning. The Administration was about to sign off on the new air-quality standards.

Browner was the first to speak. Opening the ceremony, she praised President Clinton—whom she knew was throwing a bone to Gore—and Gore, who had doggedly convinced the president to go along with her.

"These new, stronger, more protective air quality standards were made possible by the leadership, vision, and courage of the president and vice president," she said. "They stood up for the public interest. They stood up for cleaner air. They stood up for our children and their right to breathe air that does not make them sick or do long-term damage to their standards."

Hoping to shore up Gore's support among those who had questioned his hesitation, Browner assured them, "No one has a greater, more sincere, more passionate commitment to protecting public health and the environment than Vice President Gore. The vice president's wisdom and his determination to do the right thing have always guided us in the setting of important public health and environmental standards."

Browner reiterated the fantastic claim that the new standards would prevent 15,000 premature deaths, 350,000 cases of aggravated asthma, and ease breathing difficulties for more than a million children.

As if to refute any grudging doubters, the White House produced one of the 15,000 children supposed to benefit from its new policy: the asthmatic son of Sydney Lipsen-Moor of Takoma Park. Lipsen-Moor had been invited to the White House to bear testament to the ineffable burden of having to track air-quality reports to know when it was safe for her child to play outside.

After Lipsen-Moor had fully expounded on her plight, it was the vice president's turn at the podium. Gore was at his moralizing best.

> We are here today to take the most significant step in a generation to protect the American people—especially our children—from air pollution....We're taking action to improve the quality of the air we breathe and doing so in a way that makes sense for our communities, for our families, and for our economy. Most importantly, we're moving forward on our greatest challenge, and that is to provide a better and safer and healthier world for our children and their children to come.
>
> We know that people who have heart or respiratory illnesses can die an early death because of bad air. And we know that even healthy people can suffer lung damage if they exercise or work outdoors in air that, until today, they were told was perfectly safe. We now know better. The scientific evidence is in, and it needs to be updated and reflected in the way our government acts. That's why the president made the decision to update the air quality standards for smog and for soot. From this day on, those standards will reflect what we now know to be true about the dangers of polluted air....
>
> On this hot summer day, you don't have to look very far to understand that, despite the progress of the past quarter century, air pollution is still a serious problem in this country.

This is the fourth "ozone red alert day" in a row for people living in and around Washington, D.C.

Do you know what that means? It means that parents are urged to keep their kids indoors. Elderly people, and those with heart and respiratory ailments, are warned not to go outside. Even healthy people are cautioned against jogging or strenuous outdoor exercise.

Not long before, the Clinton Administration had deemed ozone at current levels insufficiently dangerous to warrant a simple measure such as keeping non-essential employees home from work for a day. Indeed, a July 17 item in *The Washington Post* quoted an administration spokesman at the Office of Personnel Management, Doug Walker, as scoffing at our request for a government shutdown. "This air quality thing," he said, "while serious, doesn't seem to justify the cost of shutting down the government." White House spokesman Mike McCurry added that given the day off, federal workers would simply have gone shopping anyway.

Yet here were Browner and Gore, announcing that air quality presented such a threat to Americans' health that citizens must spend billions more dollars to make it microscopically cleaner on normal days all over the country.

Just what we need today, I mused. More hot air out of Washington.

9. Superfund, asbestos, and other confusions

The impetus for Superfund was Love Canal, this nation's best-known hazardous waste site. From 1943 until 1952 in Niagara Falls, New York, Hooker Chemical and Plastics Corporation buried 22,000 tons of chemical waste in a half-dug canal.

When the local school board later tried to buy the land, Hooker Corporation resisted, warning of potential health hazards because of the chemicals underneath. But the school board persisted, and finally the company relented, selling the property for only $1—a means of symbolically washing its hands of future consequences.

Hooker Corporation also was adamant that the land never be excavated under any circumstances, a caveat the city ignored. Instead, it built a housing project on the land, dug through the protective clay cover over the chemicals, and laid sewer lines through the waste.

Yet residents seemingly suffered no ill effects until a reporter for the local newspaper began writing articles telling them how sick he thought they should be. Suddenly every twinge and sniffle was blamed on Love Canal. The area became a *cause celebre* for environmental extremists eager to tout the evils of the modern industrial age. "Love Canal" entered the lexicon as shorthand for toxic terror.

It was later discovered that, not people, but truth had been poisoned at Love Canal. Extensive research by both the federal and New York state governments eventually concluded that residents of Love Canal had no higher incidence of illness than people in other communities. Residents of Pocatello, Idaho, might as well have blamed their ailments on proximity to potato farms. But by the time reasonable people began suspecting the truth—that as the *New York Times* predicted in 1981, "It may well turn out that the public suffered less from the chemicals [at Love Canal] than from the hysteria generated by flimsy research irresponsibly handled"—Al Gore already had pushed through Congress the infamous Superfund law.

It has been an unqualified failure.

The statute's most egregious injustice is that it penalizes people for having engaged in perfectly lawful behavior by giving the EPA authority to declare a practice retroactively illegal. It is like putting up stop signs and then ticketing drivers for not having stopped there before the rules changed.

I objected to that non-sensical practice and told the EPA as much when the agency descended on a landfill in Buckingham County, Virginia, which had been declared a Superfund site.

From 1962 to 1982, Buckingham County Landfill was owned and operated by Joseph Love. In the beginning, Love's dump received only household garbage. But in 1977, his Sanitary Landfill Permit was modified to allow 200 gallons of "hazardous" waste per month. Two years later, the state board of health increased that to 40,000 gallons per month, and the county grew concerned. So in 1982, taxpayers bought the landfill from Love so they could close it—which they did.

The action proved the adage that no good deed goes unpunished. Four years later, the EPA, through a study local taxpayers were forced to underwrite, concluded that the site should be added to the federal Superfund list. From the name "Superfund," you might think this was some sort of a boon. What it actually meant was that taxpayers and former users—all of whom obeyed the laws as they were at the time, and had recently worked out an agreement that suited all of them—would have to spend millions of dollars cleaning up the site.

Because they took the initiative to protect their environment, in other words, the EPA was penalizing them. Had they ignored the site and let the environment degrade, the agency would have left them alone. In addition to the county and other companies, the EPA named Thomasville Furniture Company a responsible party. So, Thomasville chiefly faced substantial penalties for having lawfully discarded refuse and for having deep pockets.

"Our plan for closing the site was approved by the state and reviewed by the EPA," said the Buckingham Commonwealth's Attorney. "It never occurred to us they would eventually decide everything had to be moved from the site."

In 1993, though, that's exactly what the agency had decided. One-fourth of the contaminants it had determined were in the landfill had to be taken to another site and incinerated. The rest of the landfill was to be capped, and the contaminated groundwater pumped and treated. The EPA estimated the costs at $20 million. Others put it closer to $35 million.

According to the agency's reports, the landfill had operated by the book. The EPA's own records noted:

> In November, 1972, the Virginia State Board of Health issued a permit to the facility to dispose of municipal waste. In 1977, the permit was modified to allow the disposal of chemical wastes that a local furniture-making industry [Thomasville] generated. In 1979, the solid waste landfill operation was closed and covered to the satisfaction of the VSBH...In 1983, the county closed the hazardous waste portion in accordance with state regulations...

"I think the whole thing is enormously unfair," I said. "If the government says something is legal and you do it, is it fair to come back retroactively, imply that you have done something wrong and say 'now you're responsible for cleaning it up' and provide no assistance or incentives when what you did was perfectly legal?"

(In fact, no attorney has ever been able to give me an explanation that made clear to me how this doctrine of EPA, which has been defended in some Republican Administrations as well, can possibly be squared with the constitution's explicit protection against *ex post facto* laws. Perhaps, like the Second or Tenth Amendments, the courts have simply decided they don't like those rules and aren't going to obey them. But this doctrine of re-defining behavior as illegal after the fact is surely one of the most noxious doctrines we have. It is the essence of tyranny.)

Buckingham county officials didn't get the doctrine either. They and the other responsible parties sought a second opinion. Independent waste-disposal engineers concluded that the EPA's goals could be accomplished simply by capping the landfill and adding monitoring wells—for only $1.3 million.

The alternative was pitched to the EPA, which said it would think about it.

I didn't have to think about it too long. After meeting with the Thomasville people and the DEQ staff following the case, I concluded the EPA was being unreasonable.There w as no evidence of groundwater contamination, and Thomasville was willing to pay for additional groundwater monitors, in case any ever developed.

Nothing justified the EPA's insistence on the more expensive remedy of digging up a portion of the closed landfill and carting off the contents.

"EPA doesn't have science on its side," I argued. "Plus, if they do this, Virginia will have to stop and apprehend the EPA agents for trucking hazardous waste through town and posing a danger to the citizens, including small children."

The EPA planned a public hearing, and I made it clear that I would not be lending the power of Virginia to do the agency's dirty work. To the contrary, I said, "Virginia officials will come and be an advocate for the lower-cost remedy."

At the public hearing, with Virginia officials in attendance, the EPA modified its demands somewhat, but negotiations continued for another year. In September 1995, the other companies, excluding Thomasville, agreed to pay off the EPA with a cash settlement; the agency issued a Unilateral Administrative Order to Thomasville Furniture, saying "do it our way, or else."

By then I had more thoroughly reviewed Superfund's sorry track record. It was not reassuring.

The law had cost taxpayers and private industry $30 billion. Yet, in all those years, only 90 of the 1,300 sites had been cleaned up.

Two of those 90 sites were in Virginia, and they had been cleaned up through natural remediation, with virtually no role for Superfund.

Moreover, only half the money had gone to pay for clean-up costs. The other half had gone to employ bureaucrats administering the program and enrich lawyers fighting for or against it. Nothing against lawyers, it is just that Superfund was supposed to clean up environmental problems, not enrich lawyers.

Virginia was one of 37 states that had found we could do the job much more efficiently on our own—primarily by cutting out the expensive middle men whose every incentive was to keep their cash cow going forever.

So I decided to block adding seven more Virginia sites to the Superfund list, in accordance with an arcane provision in the law that allows the EPA to designate a Superfund site only if the governor requests it. Our administration supported efficient, effective clean up of sites returning them to beneficial uses as soon as possible. This is exactly why Governor Allen enthusiastically supported the bi-partisan Voluntary Remediation legislation in 1995 and the bill in 1997 that expanded brownfield redevelopment.

Buckingham's experience bore out my long-held thought about dealing with the EPA's bureaucracy.

It's like a casino. They really don't mind losing a hand every now and then because they know eventually they will get back everything and more. The real game is to keep the "suckers" at the table.

We decided to walk away from the federal Superfund program declining to serve as an administrative arm of EPA in Virginia. Our plan was to clean up sites through our new voluntary remediation and brownfield programs, advocate the interests of Virginians in Superfund disputes and constantly rely on sound science when considering solutions. Keeping sites off the Superfund list would allow our citizens, local governments and businesses much greater opportunities to responsibly clean the sites more quickly and cost effectively. We did add any U.S. Department of Defense sites and former federal sites that the feds were responsible for cleaning up anyway.

Like other "beneficiaries" of Superfund, the good people of Good Shepherd United Methodist Church in Dale City, Virginia, were victims of the manufactured asbestos crisis.

Even the EPA had announced, following its 1988 study, that it found indoor asbestos levels no more dangerous than the natural levels that are ubiquitous in the air and water.

Writing for the prestigious *New England Journal of Medicine*, Yale professor of medicine Dr. Bernard Gee said, "The basis for this fear is unreal, not founded in reality, a gross overreaction that's high in emotional content." There is no evidence asbestos is a public health threat, Gee said, and quoted a friend who described the phenomenon as "paratoxicology."

Though Congress took the lead on this synthetic scare by passing a law in 1987 requiring every school board in the country to come up with an asbestos-abatement plan, the EPA was ready to jump on board. When it came to writing more regulations, any excuse would do. The agency called for asbestos abatement when older buildings are renovated or demolished.

Because Good Shepherd was known to contain asbestos, every year the 500-member congregation was required to send an individual to EPA-mandated training on how to follow the latest rules regarding the non-existent threat. That was expensive; plus, the church decided to expand. So in 1992 they hired a contractor to remove the insulation.

While the project was underway, one Friday evening after the church office had closed, a man who earned extra income doing inspections for the EPA paid a surprise visit to the site and found a teaspoonful of asbestos dust in a cinder block above a door.

After he reported his findings to the EPA, the agency informed the church that this was a violation of federal clean-up regulations. Asbestos dust is supposed to be dampened to reduce ease of inhalation; failing to do so "constitutes a substantive violation of the work practice standards," the agency said—and that meant a fine of $26,000.

Good Shepherd's members were stunned. For one thing, clean-up at the construction site was the contractor's responsibility. Why would the EPA punish the church? And though the dust may have been present when the inspector visited, the building was still sealed under a plastic tent. All asbestos dust had been removed before the church was re-opened. Why such an outrageous penalty for a minor infraction that had caused no harm?

Victor Bras, chairman of the church's administrative board, first tried reasoning with the EPA, explaining that such a punitive fine would cripple the church's ministry. The $26,000 fine represented nearly a tenth of the small church's budget. "You are talking about us not being able to minister to our community," Bras explained to Peter Kostmayer's legal staff. "[The $26,000] represents that much less that we could do for the poor or the people who need counseling and help." It soon became apparent Bras might as well have been sowing grass seed in the Sahara.

"What they said to us was, 'Look, we know you guys are a church and are trying to do right, but we're going to do this because we know we can,'" Bras reported.

"They were interested in convictions and were going after institutions like ours because we can't fight back very well."

For two years, the church's lawyers tried to wrangle an agreement with the EPA, but every time they would ask for a dismissal, the agency would counter and delay. At one point, Bras, the church pastor, and the church lawyer went to see Congresswoman Leslie Byrne, who assigned a staffer to meet with them and didn't even speak as she passed through the office.

Deliverance finally came after Senator John Warner complained to Carol Browner. "This heavy-handed and insensitive treatment of the church is an example of overzealous regulation at its worst," said Warner, along with Congressman Tom Davis, who had replaced Leslie Byrne representing the 11th District.

Publicly, neither Browner nor Kostmayer budged. But after two years of administrative hearings, litigation, and lawmakers' pleas, an EPA administrative law judge dismissed the complaint against the church. The agency said it would pursue instead the engineering firm.

Bras said the church fought the EPA as much on principle as anything else. "We were making a statement that, for once, we were not going to let the EPA beat up on a small institution," he said. "We thought they were taking action that had a lot of destructive purposes. These are bureaucratic victories for them. They prey on institutions like ours."

Undoubtedly, someone at the EPA recognized what poor public relations it was for the agency to be going after a small church congregation. But how many small businesses with similarly meager resources are socked for similarly minor infractions? Congressmen don't become heroes by defending Jimbo's Bait 'n' Tackle Shop.

Good Shepherd's predicament made the papers as far away as Memphis, Tennessee, where the *Commercial Appeal* rightly noted:

A powerful federal agency that can't use a little
judgment in deciding whom to pursue poses a greater public
hazard than a few molecules of insulation.

The Voluntary Remediation Program, created by a law in 1995 was patroned by a Democratic member of the General Assembly and enthusiastically supported by the Allen Administration. It was Virginia's answer to the failed federal Superfund program.

Under this program, owners or operators of contaminated sites not mandated for remediation under existing environmental laws enter into an agreement with the state. The responsible party is required to submit three primary reports regarding planned clean-up and progress. Upon completion, the state granted immunity from future enforcement action.

Instead of simply writing a check to the state, which did nothing for the environment, owners of contaminated land could focus their energy and resources on actually improving the site and putting it back into a beneficial use.

The EPA called this "letting polluters off the hook." Most others called it common sense.

Since 1995. DEQ has negotiated voluntary remediation agreements for over fifty sites and more than fifteen have already completed their clean-up.

Following on the success of Virginia's own clean-up program, Delegate Jay Katzen worked with the Allen administration to pass a brownfield's amendment to this statute in 1997. This new law provided even greater flexibility to local governments that were interested in providing tax incentives for clean-ups of brownfields in their communities. It passed unanimously.

10. The Chesapeake Bay and Virginia's rivers

The Chesapeake Bay is one of the most important coastal estuaries in the world. It is formed from the flow of the Susquehanna and Potomac rivers and their tributaries, and is impacted by a host of other rivers and streams arising in New York, Pennsylvania, Delaware, West Virginia, Maryland and Virginia. The magnificent marine and recreational resources of the Chesapeake Bay have served as a magnet for people from the earliest of times, and great cities like Baltimore, Washington, Norfolk and even Richmond have grown up with the Chesapeake as a significant part of their respective local cultures. When people in these areas refer to "the Bay" it goes without saying that they are referring to the Chesapeake Bay. James Michener and hundreds of lesser known authors have created a extensive body of literature that celebrates just how important the Bay is to every generation.

As a consequence, the Bay is often on people's minds, and is a focus of almost everyone's interest in the environment. Virtually everyone who is active in public life and politics in the states surrounding the Bay never fails to give expression of oaths of fealty to the Bay, just as they would to the Flag, and to mom and apple pie. Yet in the decades prior to the 1980's the Bay was so demonstrably resilient to vigorous use over the centuries that people took it for granted and it began to suffer from what is often called "the tragedy of the commons." That is, everyone uses it but as it belongs to no one, we all assume that someone else is taking care of it. The degradation of the quality and condition of the Bay began to be remedied when public officials joined together in 1983 to form a voluntary partnership committed to "taking ownership" and responsibility for the Bay. The Chesapeake Bay Program partners were the U.S. Environmental Protection Agency, the

District of Colombia, and the representatives of the governments of Pennsylvania, Maryland and Virginia. If ever there were genuine bipartisan and generally cooperative efforts to improve environmental quality, the sundry efforts to rescue the Chesapeake Bay would have to be counted among their number.

Just after I was confirmed as Secretary of Natural Resources in January 1994, one of the Committees of the multi-state Bay program held a regularly scheduled meeting in Lancaster, Pennsylvania. Because the Virginia General Assembly was in full swing, commanding my constant presence and attention, and because the new Allen Administration had not yet had an opportunity to put together its complement of key leaders and representatives, I asked my husband, George, to attend the Lancaster meeting as a volunteer and my personal representative. I wanted to demonstrate to the other states that Virginia placed a high priority on efforts to improve the quality of the Bay. George came to the mission with significant credentials, as he had been one of the sub-Cabinet officers in the Reagan Administration whose agencies had responsibility for elements of the federal commitment to the Bay program. Over the years he had developed personal relationships with many of the participants and was warmly welcomed by the group when he related the purpose of his mission there.

By late March of 1994, the General Assembly had concluded its biannual session and I had been able to personally attend a subsequent meeting of the multi-state commission and now had been briefed on the activities of myriad other Chesapeake Bay committees, commissions and agencies, including one of the Agencies under my Secretariat with the endearing name of CBLAD, or the Chesapeake Bay Local Assistance Department.

On April 7, out of the sky-blue I received a letter from William Matuszeski, the Director of the Chesapeake Bay Program of the Environmental Protection Agency. It read in part,

> "It was a pleasure to meet you and to work with you at the recent meeting of the Principals' Staff Committee of the Chesapeake Bay Program. We at the Bay Program Office especially appreciated your enthusiasm about the Chesapeake, as well as your willingness to review the work underway and to develop the commonwealth's role in the Bay's restoration under your leadership."
>
> Matuszeski went on to remind me about the several million dollars EPA provides to the states to meet Program objectives. And, how nutrient reduction strategies of the various states were to have been completed in August of 1993 but that they were taking longer than expected, "in part due to extensive efforts to engage the public in their development."
>
> And, it continued, "To some extent, Virginia has been a special case from the beginning with respect to the tributary strategies. There has been recognition of the limited role played by the James, the York and the Rappahannock" rivers. "At the same time, the need to move quickly on a strategy for the Virginia portion of the Potomac has been paramount..."
>
> Then came the point of Matusezeski's letter. "EPA has tried to be flexible...[but] our final grant guidance ties funding...to the completion of draft strategies or satisfactory progress in their development...in order to avoid delay in the award of these grants, it would be helpful to receive by May 1 information concerning your plans and projections for these tributary strategies."

Whoa! A threat from EPA that the Allen Administration was expected to accomplish in less than one month what the previous Administration had not completed.

This did not seem like a cooperative partnership to me.

Bill Matuszeski, a bespectacled long-time career bureaucrat who was always cheerful and friendly personally, was a wily operator with an agenda to exercise and expand the Federal role in the cooperative, multi-jurisdictional partnership, and with no hesitation to use the press to communicate that agenda to state officials and the public they served. Further, he had his post at the behest of Carol Browner and was well aware of her predilection to reward and punish both EPA employees and state officials to make them compliant to her will. So, when Matuszeski assured me in the telephone call I placed to him upon receiving his letter (and following press inquiries we were receiving about "EPA threats to cut-off Virginia funds for non-compliance") that his correspondence to me was not intended by him, nor should it be regarded by me, he said, as a threat to Virginia nor heavy-handed, I accepted his assertion. But the media didn't play it that way. The *Washington Post* headline blared, "EPA Warns Virginia on Bay Clean-Up Plan." I vowed to myself to keep a wary eye on this situation as we moved ahead, as it goes without saying that it was not my office that papered the media with the EPA missive.

Quite apart from this initial exchange, our Administration's commitment to the Chesapeake and indeed all of Virginia's waterways was firm and we would proceed with Allen initiatives on our timetable. My response to EPA and the public after detailed briefings from staff of the three Virginia agencies, which had Chesapeake Bay responsibilities, was straightforward and communicated directly to the Bay Program office in an official letter and in a public release to the citizens of Virginia.

Our message was that Governor Allen had voiced his commitment to the improvement of the Chesapeake Bay (during his campaign and following his inauguration) and our Administration would seek innovative ways to enhance this important resource. I stated that our commitments would move forward with the appropriate course of action on each of the Bay rivers affected.

It should be noted that the Bay Program's 1992 modeling study showed that Virginia's rivers below the Potomac—the Rappahannock, James, York and smaller coastal rivers—do not contribute significantly to the excess nutrient problems of the main stem of the Bay...whereas the Potomac and rivers northward in Maryland and the Susquehanna do cause more significant problems.

...scientific data indicates that Virginia's rivers...have some dissolved oxygen problems...and we are moving forward with additional water quality monitoring on our rivers below the Potomac to give us a clearer picture of what improvements in water quality are needed.

I acknowledged previous Bay program dollars to Virginia and indicated that as a result of the money received in November of 1993, additional water quality monitoring was being done on these rivers since January 1994. Twenty-six new water quality sites were added on the three rivers in order to get a more complete picture of the water conditions in the rivers themselves.

The monitoring data will then be factored into a computer model for each river. The model (another EPA model) will enable us to predict how water quality conditions might improve if certain actions are taken. Sound science and resource conservation practices will drive Virginia's policies and deeds to improve the environment—inaccurate and overblown newspaper headlines will not.

I restated our commitment to continuing our cooperative relationship with our sister states in the Bay Program, and with the federal EPA and other agencies *to integrate strategies that are most effective for Virginia* (emphasis mine) with those of the other states.

Three other points I made at the time would have tremendous impact on our work. One, we determined that our Administration would educate, involve and cooperate with citizens of the Commonwealth on the development of our strategies. Two, that the Allen Administration was operating under serious fiscal constraints and that we would carefully consider all the options and impacts before finalizing a plan. And, three, that the James, York and Rappahannock plans would be based on EPA modeling which Matuszeski advised me would be completed in 1997.

Press stories were written that EPA prompting had caused us to move forward. I certainly didn't agree with that spin, but must concede that EPA has a very good press operation and seems to believe in the use of the hammer of always threatening to withhold funds from a state as a way of grabbing headlines and exercising its dominance over the states. It was a very useful political tool for the agency, and when considered in the context of the same tactics used by other divisions of EPA, can only be regarded as the modus operandi of the Clinton-Gore-Browner way of governance.

The *Virginia Pilot* reported that "...the state will begin a series of public hearings on run-off pollution in September [1994]. A plan to reduce the problem is expected to be finished sometime after 1997."

EPA officials were quoted as saying that the state was now on track. It was July.

And Joe Maroon, Virginia director of the activist Chesapeake Bay Foundation, even expressed his cautious optimism. "We think it's an encouraging sign that the Allen Administration has indicated an effort to move forward," Maroon said. "It's a team approach and we need all players as a team to participate if it's going to be successful."

The *Washington Times* ran an AP report that described a sparring match between Virginia and the EPA and reported that the Virginia delay in submitting its plan for EPA review was the result of foot-dragging in the waning months of Gov. L. Douglas Wilder's Administration, plus the start-up time needed for Gov. George Allen's Administration. It certainly was true that the Allen team had our plates full with General Assembly activities, budget revisions, bill review of hundreds of pieces of legislation introduced by state legislators, personnel interviews and decisions, program reviews and many, many meetings with citizens who were eager to meet the new management in state government and to communicate their ideas and frustrations.

Oh yes...and then the AP story noted our struggle with EPA over centralized auto emission inspections in Northern Virginia and reported that "there was a concern" that Virginia was just trying to "pick [another] fight."

Well, not exactly.

172

I had recruited my Deputy Secretary Tom Hopkins from his private law practice in Roanoke. He had interned for Senator Robert Byrd during his college days in West Virginia, served on the staff of the Commander in Chief of the Atlantic Fleet in the Navy, and then went to work as an attorney in private business. After serving for a number of years in management and as in-house counsel for three major natural resource companies, as well as further serving his country during a ten-year stint in the active Army Reserves in the Judge Advocate General Corps, he had returned home to Roanoke to be near his aging parents. Having set up a small law practice, he further contributed to his community by serving on the adjunct faculty of a local college and as an administrative hearing officer for the Supreme Court of Virginia.

Tom stood nearly 6 foot 2 and weighed about 300 pounds, had a graying beard, horn rimmed glasses and a very gentle manner, just like Grizzly Adams. He told me when we first met that he was not an experienced government person but he just wanted to come and offer his services to Governor Allen. His corporate work had dealt with many EPA regulations and resource issues and his legal experience as well as environmental work made him an ideal deputy for me. Governor Allen agreed with my recommendation and appointed Tom Deputy Secretary.

He started work on June 17, 1994, and among his duties were to oversee the Chesapeake Bay tributary project for my office, coordinating the several state agencies that were active in matters that directly affected the Chesapeake Bay program, and from which we drew teams for each tributary system. We called these people our Trib Teams.

Tom and I determined that our highest priority would be to focus first on the Potomac River, because Virginia had committed in previous years to reduce the nutrients flowing into the Bay from the Potomac by 40 percent by the year 2000. I needed to select a team of people willing to work long hours with the many local government officials and citizens we intended to include in this decision process. We were convinced that the key to continued

Bay success was for as many people and jurisdictions as possible to take "ownership" of the Bay to overcome the "tragedy of the commons." Hopkins and I carefully identified the state agencies that we wanted to be sure were involved and then began to map out our strategy for bringing this plan to fruition.

My lead agency would be the Chesapeake Bay Local Assistance Department or CBLAD. Established by the General Assembly, CBLAD had always been a stepchild agency. I determined, however, that by making this agency the lead, the Allen Administration would boldly proclaim that we intended to champion the Bay and put at the forefront the only agency that had the Bay as its sole focus. I also hoped that this would demonstrate to Tayloe Murphy, the state delegate who had willed CBLAD into existence, that we intended to elevate "his" agency to a higher status than had any other Governor or Secretary of Natural Resources. This decision was not without internal debate and discussion as other agencies in my Secretariat made the case for their leadership role in what they knew would be an important priority for the Allen Administration. Among people who follow such matters, our decision to put the responsibility in a heretofore virtually ignored agency, in the face of internal lobbying from other agencies with earnest patrons in the General Assembly, was keenly watched.

Later, when our Administration proposed to the General Assembly formalizing this arrangement by combining all the Bay programs into CBLAD, it was reported to me that Joe Maroon, the environmental activist who headed up the Chesapeake Bay Foundation, and who had formerly worked for JLARC, was very pleased at our decision in favor of CBLAD, but told associates that he would decline to offer public expressions of support because he didn't want to be caught giving credibility to this Bay initiative that might seem supportive of Becky Norton Dunlop and George Allen.

And I recruited the perfect person to lead CBLAD and the Bay initiatives. Mrs. Kathleen Lawrence had served in the federal government for Presidents Nixon, Ford, Reagan and Bush. One of her major management assignments had been as Deputy Under Secretary of the Department of Agriculture. She is an effervescent person who relishes challenges, loves people and had earned a reputation as a talented, efficient manager. And, she was a no-nonsense advocate for Virginia. She would represent Virginia at interstate Bay meetings that I could not attend, making sure Virginia views were presented and that Virginia appointees to Bay program committees were always alerted to meetings, offered briefings, and backed up in their work with the EPA and other states' officials. Her agriculture experience was invaluable because our work needed to be carried out with rural Virginians as well as urban and suburban citizens and local government officials. She was sensitive to their concerns and unheralded stewardship. My office also worked through her agency to set up meetings for the Trib Teams and me with local officials, local media and the public.

Our plan was to go to every local community in the Potomac watershed. This would take us from the Northern Neck in the coastal plain where the Potomac flowed into the Chesapeake Bay to the communities of the mountainous Shenandoah Valley through which the Shenandoah River arose and flowed to the Potomac. Six public meetings were held in the Shenandoah-Potomac Basin to provide information to citizens and respond to questions and concerns.

Then in early 1995, I personally went to each region to explain the state's commitment to nutrient reduction to the local governing officials and the local Soil and Water Conservation district officials and to ask them to develop a plan for their locality that would be practical and cost effective. Always, the Trib Team for that region would accompany me. It was these individuals who would work more closely with the local people responding to scientific questions, giving advice and counsel on best management practices and ultimately putting pen to paper to record the community developed plans. Governor Allen was strongly committed to local input and was determined that unfunded mandates would not be imposed on the communities that would make commitments to reduce nutrient runoff. We did not have a blank check for the plans so we emphasized the need for practicality, cost-effectiveness and local commitment for implementation.

We were pleased that local officials were responsive to the concept of their "taking ownership" for the contributions that were being made to water degradation in their jurisdictions that ultimately contributed adversely to water quality in the Bay. Contributing to this support from locally elected officials, most of whom were Democrats, was their understanding that we were steadfast in making it known that George Allen would not send legislation to the General Assembly that would impose unfunded mandates on their communities...and George Allen and I were steadfast to that commitment.

This "Trib Strategy" initiative was very exciting but fraught with peril. One of the state employees from the Department of Conservation and Recreation repeatedly stated to anyone who would listen his conviction that local government officials in Virginia would never do anything without being forced into it by the state. Needless to say, I disagreed with him but we continued to include him in the process for a time until finally he so infuriated his colleagues on the Trib Team that he was assigned other responsibilities and eventually left state government. The local officials had every right to be skeptical of our approach when they found themselves with civil servants with attitudes like that. An additional challenge for us was their one constant question...will these plans become mandatory? My response: "Not on George Allen's watch, they won't! We are committed to being true partners and we believe that the people of Virginia care about the health of their rivers...and healthy rivers mean a healthy Bay."

In October 1994, Governor Allen had been elected by his peers to be Chairman of the Chesapeake Bay Executive Council. He led the initiatives during his tenure to require that local government officials from all jurisdictions be included in future

176

deliberations before commitments were made by Governors that would mandate unfunded programs onto the citizens. While all this was going on, the activist Chesapeake Bay Foundation spent its time caterwauling over details, such as distinctions between "making the Bay free from toxic chemicals" and "making the Bay free from the *impact* of toxic chemicals." The Foundation was alarmed at Allen's strategy against unfunded state and federal mandates on local communities and his pledge to endorse the rights of private property owners to assure they are compensated when environmental laws restrict the use of their land.

Even Maryland's Democratic Governor, Parris Glendening, got into the drama. Locked into a difficult campaign challenge, Glendening sought to strengthen his environmental credentials by telling an editorial board of the *Washington Post* that he was concerned that the Republican governors of Pennsylvania and Virginia were backing off from protecting the Bay, and that he would hope to use his "personal persuasion and personal interaction" to increase Virginia's environmental commitment. (Of course, the irony is that Maryland has endured one water quality crisis after another under Glendening's leadership— situations that never reached crisis proportions in Virginia: *pfiesteria* outbreaks; algae blooms in the upper Bay; dredge spoils dumping in environmentally sensitive locations, and severe environmental violations of the Potomac River water quality, habitat, endangered species and federal laws in advancing development of the National Harbor project and the replacement of the Wilson Bridge.) The *Washington Post* headline, "Allen to Head Bay Clean-Up Program" referring in part to Glendening, was obligingly sublined, "Environmentalists Fear Va. Governor Will Slow Regional Effort." Just as had been reported to me months earlier, the Democratic "loyal opposition," their handmaidens in the media, and the activist organizations were determined to complain about any effort that might inure to the positive environmental reputation of the Allen Administration.

One very important component of our strategic partnership was the system of Soil and Water Conservation Districts. There are about 45 of these throughout Virginia, and there are commensurate Districts in all the other states. District commissioners are elected by the general population and serve without pay. Often they are provided technical and logistic support from the USDA's Soil Conservation Service and from funds appropriated by County governments.

A farmer in Bath County, Edward T. Walters, wrote a commentary in the *Roanoke Times and World-News* in March of 1994 about the great potential of the Soil and Water Districts. I agreed with many of the points he made and discussed with my husband George his own very favorable experience with the national programs of the Soil and Water Conservation Districts during his tenure as Assistant Secretary of Agriculture. For my entire tenure, I looked for ways to increase the influence and leadership of the Districts in water quality and other resource management projects of the Allen Administration. I was thoroughly committed to their involvement in the development of these tributary strategies.

One initiative our Administration advanced would have put these Soil and Water District officials in charge of at least 75% of the dollars raised through the sale of Virginia auto tags with a Chesapeake Bay theme. At that time, the revenue generated by these special license plates was put in a fund at the Department of Environment Quality with the usual intent that a centralized group in Richmond would parcel out the dollars as they saw fit. Our plan was to return money to the Soil and Water Conservation District organizations where the license plates had been sold. The result would be that those districts that encouraged their citizens to purchase Bay plates would have a substantial sum of money to spend on projects to improve the Bay. They could use the money in their district, they could provide it to another community that sought financial assistance for a good project, or they could combine resources with other districts for an even larger project.

178

To my way of thinking, this would ensure that citizens buying these license plates would see more of their intent realized in their own community and through the guidance of their locally elected officials. I thought it would also build stronger relationships between communities if the Soil and Water Conservation Districts were working closely with each other on projects that would benefit water quality and each had its own pot of money.

Alas, no sooner had I laid out the plan in a speech in January 1995, had received positive feedback from a number of district officials with the requisite request for more details, and left the meeting than word came back that certain environmental activists had put out the word that environmental organizations should veto this idea…. "Can't put this much money in the hands of the district leaders," they warned. It must be left in a centralized account in Richmond to be parceled out by a committee controlled by the state, where the activist organizations could weigh in to get some of the money for their activism. As it turned out, the General Assembly took the activists' counsel and simply appropriated the Chesapeake license plate fund to itself for General Assembly staff to drive the distribution—not the Soil and Water Conservation Districts. Governor Allen was very philosophical about this aborted initiative…I was sad. I had believed that these Soil and Water Conservation District elected officials were worthy of this opportunity and was truly disappointed that General Assembly members did not and even some of the locally elected Soil and Water District officials themselves did not. I pulled out my Edward Walters piece to re-energize my thinking as to why I should be promoting more money and more authority for the Soil and Water Districts. There would be other opportunities…our Trib Strategy was certainly one.

One of the best examples of work by local Soil and Water Conservation Districts to benefit the Potomac Tributary strategy is a publication by the Potomac Basin Soil and Water Conservation Districts in Northern Virginia published in July 1997. Entitled *You and Your Land, A Homeowner's Guide for the Potomac River Watershed*, it is a very user-friendly 78-page primer that provides important, practical information to every homeowner concerned about how their lifestyle choices impact on the river and tributaries they so enjoy in their community. In the introductory acknowledgments section, it is noted that they contracted with Lardner/Klein Landscape Architects to write the text and produce the illustrations and charts, Kristen Mosbaek Communications to design the publication and a listing of individuals for their contributions to the book. I could only wistfully imagine how public "ownership" of the Bay would have been enhanced if only they had been able to thank the many citizens from their Districts who purchased Bay license plates for their contribution to the community wide efforts, instead of the Richmond crowd who dispensed grant money. A wonderful project, an excellent publication, fine leadership, and a lost opportunity to directly connect the stewardship investment of the people with the beneficial results of an improved Potomac watershed.

Despite this setback and missed opportunity we never veered from our determined track to advance the Potomac Tributary Strategy, and we progressed steadily. Local officials are often active business people, farmers, or with other fixed employment commitments in addition to being elected officials. Of course, these kind of folk are a bit more difficult to gather together for a presentation from state officials than are people who are paid to work full-time for the government or who are full time activists. So it required great perseverance and endurance as we methodically worked our way through the watershed to meet with local government officials, their staff and citizens.

Local meetings always included a presentation of the EPA computer modeling results that established the need for a 40% reduction in nutrients in the Potomac River watershed. There were frequent questions about the modeling, a tool many find difficult to accept as a basis for the often extraordinary and expensive changes sought to bring locales into compliance with the computer's results. DEQ, DCR and CBLAD officers and staff did their best to respond to questions from the local officials and citizens. Always, there was discussion about what the source of most of the nutrients was, where the nutrient loading was most likely to have occurred and what efforts other communities were discussing as possible plans to meet the 40% reduction objective. Because each Trib Team worked together as a true team in each and every jurisdiction to which they traveled, and because the state was committed to openness and transparency, the discussions became easier even when the answers were difficult to explain.

Our Interagency Staff Group developed a questionnaire for local government officials to determine what activities were already underway in communities. Again, the goal was to achieve the 40% nutrient reduction by having everyone in the watershed do their fair share. If some communities had already put programs in place to reduce nutrient loading, it was our intention to make certain those actions were recorded and the communities received credit for their efforts rather than asking them to do more than others who had not achieved as much nutrient reduction. All the information would be compiled by the state—working closely with the local officials—and then it would become apparent where more action was needed. The objective was to develop a Tributary Nutrient Reduction Strategy put together by the communities. The process of the explanatory meetings, completing the question-naires, compiling the data, and reviewing the compiled material, took about one year from mid-1994 to mid-1995.

It was a lot of hard work. It was easy to understand why the activists preferred to deal with a handful of government employees centralized in Richmond or to have only to lobby a few of the most powerful members of the General Assembly. I had always wondered what drove liberal activists to be such adherents of central planning and control, and I came to learn that while part of their conviction often rested in certain socialistic ideological tendencies, another part might be evidence that they are just too plain lazy to want to work the precincts like we did with the Trib Strategy in those years.

Soon enough the August 1995 draft document was written. Now it would be taken once again to another round of public meetings in the Shenandoah and Potomac River Basins so citizens could review it and ask questions of the state officials who again went with me to each area to introduce the strategy. It was important to stay in touch with the public and the various communities every step of the way if we intended to keep them on board with our goals. And we were determined to do that.

The goal of this second round of meetings would be to work through potential local commitments in the four regions of the basin relying on voluntary actions. We worked through the challenges one might expect: the urban counties wanted rural counties to do more; rural counties want to be certain that in the urban counties, run-off from housing developments was included and waste-water treatment plants were held accountable; every local official, as I recall, wanted to be re-assured that the state would do its share and would work to assure that everyone else would do their share; and some just disagreed with the EPA model that generated the 40% reduction agreement.

The Trib Teams did the intensive labor of working through these issues with the staff of local governments, including municipalities, soil and water conservation districts, wastewater service authorities, and planning district commissions in the Basin. Many meetings were held to reach agreement on assessment of activities in place and underway and then to discuss financing alternatives to implement desirable plans.

A key element of our Potomac strategy included fixing the chronic problems associated with the Blue Plains wastewater treatment plant owned by the District of Columbia. This was important in the Virginia strategy because Blue Plains handles Virginia sewage to the tune of about 40% of its business. If this plant alone were upgraded to remove nutrients, it would amount to such a huge reduction that the rest of our plan would be much more easy to achieve. Without the Blue Plains reduction, there would be no way that Virginia could achieve its goal. The sticking point was state and federal cost share payments or related grants.

Virginia counties Fairfax and Loudoun would have to increase their ratepayers' utility fees to help upgrade the Blue Plains plant. They wanted some assurance of state cost sharing. I knew this upgrade must be included in the Virginia strategy since Blue Plains handled so much of Northern Virginia's wastewater.

Our Tributary Strategy process was moving along systematically. While it was time-consuming to hold the many meetings we did, it was critical to stay in regular communication with local communities, to be responsive to their questions and suggestions and maintain the partnership we were building. The Interagency team was working very well, too. I had been warned about the conflicts that often occurred between state agencies but I must say that without regard to any past circumstances, these team members were very professional in their approach to the project and to their dealings with each other. Other agencies in addition to CBLAD, DEQ and DCR that significantly contributed to the project included the Virginia Marine Resources Commission, the Department of Game and Inland Fisheries, the Virginia Institute of Marine Sciences, the Department of Agriculture, and the Department of Forestry.

In January 1996, I appointed team leaders for the Rappahannock, York and James Rivers, and we began our tributary strategy development for those rivers. The Chesapeake Bay Program was scheduled to complete its expansion and refinement of the watershed and water quality models in the spring of 1997. This was a necessary step to establish site and situation specific goals for nutrient reduction in each of lower tributary basins. The General Assembly incorporated the Commonwealth's tributary strategies program into state law during its 1996 session.

On March 7, I released a report to the public and to the General Assembly entitled *Chesapeake Bay and Its Tributaries: Results of Monitoring Programs and Status of Resources*. The report was not technical (although the technical data was on file) but was intended to provide information about the status of water quality conditions and living resources. As I pointed out at the time, "The empirical evidence of the monitoring programs shows the estuary, though impacted, is improving and responding to sound conservation management strategies."

Outlined in the report were initiatives that our Administration cheered: the Local Government Partnership Initiative Directive that Governor Allen had led as Chairman of the Chesapeake Bay Program's Executive Council. This required that state governments inform and include local government officials in setting goals for the Bay program before decisions are made and announced to the public. Also included were provisions for agriculture producers to implement Best Management Practices voluntarily; the Virginia Poultry Federation's initiative to incorporate nutrient management planning into the operations of the producers of the four major poultry processors; preparation and distribution of sound fertilization practices to non-farmers through twelve major retailers; voluntary regulations to govern nutrient management training and certification; formation of a Virginia Forest Riparian Task Force to educate the public about and promote streamside buffers.

Each of these initiatives had at least one thing in common—its progress could be measured and each would have a positive impact on the water quality of Virginia.

As we were finishing the first tributary strategy, other programs were underway. CBLAD managed a "BayWise Home Expo" at a large metropolitan shopping mall in the Richmond area. The Expo exposed thousands of shoppers who lived in the Bay watershed to innovative technologies, products and services that would help them to be better stewards of the Bay in their own backyards. Going to the people instead of making them come to us proved to be a very popular strategy and demonstrated to citizens that government could be helpful to them in their personal endeavors to improve the environment. We also awarded "Friend of the Bay" citations to citizens who were identified as undertaking particular deeds that benefited the Bay. Authorized by the General

Assembly, I was informed that the intent was to give one award a year to someone who really deserved it. My philosophy always was to involve more people, not fewer, in our programs and to extol positive actions that would likely result in more deeds being done by more people. I also promoted oyster gardening as a wonderful way citizens could improve the water quality of the Bay and its tributaries. In fact, students near Virginia Beach each earned a "Friend of the Bay" award for their class oyster-gardening project. Those students deserved rewards and those awards will remain meaningful, as they become young adults in the Bay watershed. Another initiative was "Businesses for the Bay." Governor Allen announced this voluntary program for businesses to participate in and to encourage pollution prevention strategies and techniques. People are the most important resource and we intended that they be encouraged in every way.

The Final Comment Draft for the Shenandoah-Potomac Strategy was completed in October 1996. We gave it wide distribution since it represented such an enormous commitment for the people of Virginia. Copies were mailed to members of the county boards of supervisors, city and town councils, and directors of the soil and water conservation districts in the Shenandoah and Virginia portion of the Potomac River basins. It was distributed to members of the House Committee on the Chesapeake Bay and its Tributaries, the Senate Committee on Agriculture, Conservation and Natural Resources, the House Committee on Appropriations, the Senate Committee on Finance, the Virginia delegation to the Chesapeake Bay Commission and the Virginia Chesapeake Bay Partnership Council. And we gave out hundreds of copies to interested citizens and organizations. We made copies available for review at state DEQ and DCR offices in the Basin, Planning District Offices, Soil and Water Conservation District offices...and on the Internet. In addition, we hosted five public open houses that we held in every region of the basin on November 12, 13, 14, 18, and 20. At these open houses, which lasted from three to four hours, there were staff members, poster and other display materials to provide information to citizens with special orientation discussions offered each hour. Written comments were solicited from all interested parties with a deadline of December 2 so we could finalize the strategy and submit it to the 1997 General Assembly session along with Governor Allen's budget proposal.

It is important to note that of the four regions in the Shenandoah-Potomac Basin, only Northern Virginia came up significantly short in its goal to reach a 40% reduction. Two points must be made, however, to explain this. One, Northern Virginia had done a considerable amount of nutrient reduction prior to 1985, the year that the Bay Program Executive Council chose for its baseline in 1987. Second, urban non-point reduction is difficult—excessive lawn fertilization, stormwater run-off, etc.—and is more costly to implement.

The final plan had a price tag of $95 to $100 million and we knew we had a plan that every jurisdiction had committed to achieving—if we could come up with the money. It did, however, come up 4% short of our goal of a 40% reduction. Estimates to close that gap using current technologies came in at an additional $34 to $67 million. My team struggled with the strategy to close the gap, which was to implement nutrient removal technology at all of the larger municipal wastewater treatment facilities across the Shenandoah-Potomac basin. The local officials in the Shenandoah Valley and the Lower Potomac region did not support this strategy but it was the only thing left to do. So we put them in the plan knowing that they were opposed, noting that these should be done last and were the least cost-effective projects in the strategy. We strongly believed that new technologies would come on line before this part of the plan could be implemented, thus reducing costs per unit of reduction. And, we felt the concept of nutrient trading that we had introduced in the process would eventually become accepted and used. Other issues of concern to our local partners were accommodated in the strategy and we expected these elements would become law when this strategy was approved by the General Assembly.

The Governor announced this Chesapeake Bay tributary legislative initiative in December. It was the Commonwealth's first major investment toward implementing the Shenandoah and Potomac Tributary Nutrient Reduction Strategy. Allen's initiative also proposed a first year funding request for $11 million for a new fund, the Chesapeake Bay Tributaries Restoration Trust Fund. Additionally, he proposed $8 million for the Virginia Wastewater Revolving Loan Fund that would leverage $44 million for municipal wastewater treatment plants and other water quality upgrades. All of this was in addition to the some $124 million in state and federal already being spent in Virginia for Bay-related programs and activities.

The General Assembly took a different route, declining to focus on the Chesapeake Bay, passing instead the Water Quality Improvement Act that expanded the program to all rivers in the Commonwealth, providing $15 million in funding and $8 million for the revolving loan fund, to be available throughout the state.

My Deputy Secretary, Brian Mannix (Tom Hopkins had moved to head the Department of Environmental Quality in June 1996) had a scientific background and economics training. He had worked in the Executive Office of the President at the Office of Management and Budget just a few years prior to this. I had recruited him from private business and he enthusiastically joined the Administration though there were fewer than eighteen months remaining. He eagerly took over the Interagency Staff Committee leadership on the Tributary Strategies and was an integral part of the team bringing that first strategy to completion.

On March 20, 1997, Governor Allen signed the Assembly's version of the water quality bill into law at Buckroe Beach in Hampton, Virginia. It was a blustery, cold day that was ushering in spring and this new initiative had as its core that first Tributary Strategy. Once again, an Allen environmental initiative was put into play. It was satisfying to see.

Now, with the new Water Quality Improvement Act to implement, I asked Brian to lead that project to assure that the regulations and initial grants would be completed in a timely manner. The Allen Administration had one year left and I knew that Brian could deliver a complete package consistent with the goals we had set forth when we began the tributary strategy process. It was true that the new bill expanded the water quality program statewide but the Allen Administration still would be held accountable for the Bay Tributary strategy implementation too.

Virginia's economy was strong. As we all now know, a growing economy means increased tax revenues. As 1997 progressed, Governor Allen realized that his policies were going to provide him the funding needed to keep the Shenandoah-Potomac strategy on track...and to offer him the opportunity to approve initiatives that would accelerate our nutrient reduction efforts so that Virginia could indeed meet the 40% goal. He announced at the 1997 Chesapeake Bay Executive Council Meeting on October 30 that he would propose in his 1998 budget a $60 million initiative that would enable Virginia to meet its commitment to reduce nutrient loadings into the Chesapeake Bay by 40% by the year 2000. It was a tremendous achievement, made possible by the economic growth that the environmental activists fear.

The team that had begun the Tributary process with me in 1994 and now included Brian Mannix and the new director of CBLAD, Michael Clower, signed a memorandum to the Governor on December 3, 1997 that laid out a $63.1 million budget proposal. The memo advised the Governor "...that Virginia's nutrient reduction goal of 40 percent by 2000 can be achieved by this program, and that it cannot be achieved for less." It made clear that the cooperation of all our partners was necessary for success but that could be expected. And, "Finally, the success of this program will depend on the commitment of the General Assembly to its objectives....Any dilution of the effort to achieve nutrient reduction in the Shenandoah-Potomac will be at the price of missing Virginia's commitment to reach the 40 percent goal."

Governor Allen accepted that recommendation and included the entire budget amount that the team recommended in his final budget package. He announced the first grants on November 10, 1997.

Of course, we did not ignore other rivers in the Commonwealth during this intense Bay project. There were programs and initiatives that provided opportunity to improve water quality everywhere. Evidence of this is that of the 29,000 river miles monitored in Virginia with water quality monitoring stations that increased in number from 896 to 1,114 since 1994. Nearly 95 percent of the miles monitored met or exceeded clean water standards established by EPA. The average in the United States is around 70 percent.

One of these water quality initiatives was a volunteer initiative called Fall River Renaissance. This was the autumn version of Operation Spruce-Up, our springtime initiative to get Virginians involved in good natural resource stewardship projects. The Fall River Renaissance focused on water quality. Governor Allen and I led a number of outings with students and concerned citizens planting riparian buffers. One project on the Northern Neck included prisoners working in our ConServ Virginia program planting riparian buffers with the Governor. Over 11,000 volunteers participated in Fall River Renaissance activities working somewhere in Virginia on various projects that would improve our water quality.

Another effort to involve citizens was our initiative to formalize a program to encourage citizen water quality monitoring. I visited with a number of students and teachers interested in testing water quality in their communities and providing results to the state. DEQ resisted using the information because of the uncertainty of how the tests were conducted and the accuracy of the data collected. I directed the DEQ to establish a program to train interested Virginians in how to collect information that would be useful to DEQ. This way, we could involve citizens but the

DEQ professionals would establish the protocols. We finalized the program just before we left office and it continues to this day.

As I began to think about wrapping up our work on water quality improvement, it occurred to me that if what we had accomplished were to have a lasting impact it would be important to have a credible independent science-based assessment of what was achieved. My goal was to determine what was being done well and what needed improvement.

To this end, I arranged for the Institute of Regulatory Science to undertake an independent scientific peer review of our water program for the Commonwealth. The review panels began in October 1997 and concluded their work in January 1998. The final document is entitled *Peer Review Report: Water Quality Program of the Department of Natural Resources of the Commonwealth of Virginia.* The report gave very high marks for the substance of our water programs and favorably assessed the decentralization of DEQ as well as our initiative to decentralize the Department of Conservation and Recreation soil and water program. It was published and I was able to transmit it to the General Assembly on my last day in the office.

I felt gratified for myself and my team that our service to Virginia was found to have stood well the test of science-based assessment and evaluation. I knew the success we achieved and documented would give confidence to my successors in Virginia and my colleagues in other states.

11. Clearing the Air

(Environmentalism as if clean
air, water, and soil mattered)

Both in the campaign and in his early addresses as Governor, George Allen set forth a clear vision for Virginia government. Not everyone agreed with that vision. Even critics agreed, however, that it was straightforward and specific.

Allen set forth the proposition that the federal government had grown too large, and was intruding into the lives of average Americans too much. Allen wanted to reassert the spirit of the Tenth Amendment's promise that powers not specifically given to the federal government were reserved respectively to the states and the people—to restore the federalism envisioned by the founders.

Above all, we believed in people and in government as their servant. With the right positive incentives, the overwhelming majority of the people could be expected to comport themselves in a civil and public spirited manner.

To a greater extent than I think many environmental extremists realize, George Allen and those he brought into Virginia government believe people are fundamentally pro-environment. And we thought of ourselves as the conservationist branch of environmentalists, though in our brand of environmentalism, there was a moderation regarding the means, as well as a focus on the actual ends of policy: "Clearing the air," water, and ground, as that *Richmond Times-Dispatch* headline put it not long after we left office.

In so doing, Virginia offered substantively different policies than the conventional wisdom expected, making it a laboratory which other states could emulate or shun as they preferred. And, in defending our right to do so in the face of vigorous hostility from the Environmental Protection Agency and others, we helped, I believe, to make it more possible for other states to pursue their own course—whether it resembled ours or not.

In this sense, Virginia's experience is doubly important—it was both a political and a policy departure. I was proud to be part of this endeavor, especially with the outstanding people I got to work with throughout Allen's Administration. All of this, however, only makes the Virginia experience worth looking at—not necessarily worth emulating.

What, one may fairly ask, were the results?

One result was that the policies matched our rhetoric. As George Allen likes to say, "Promises made, promises kept!" This is not the ultimate purpose of environmental policy, which is to improve the environment. It is, however, a significant result for the democratic system. If more elected officials were to run on, articulate, and then implement policies based upon a consistent philosophy, there might be a good deal less cynicism about democracy than we see today.

George Allen was able to streamline government and make it more businesslike and more responsive. Our spending on the Department of Environmental Quality was well under the original $100 million budgeted for it in each of the four years.

(Our critics claimed our efforts to strive for efficient and less costly government would gut the environment. That is an argument that must be considered, as it is below. For now, I am merely observing that we did what we said we would do to make government run at a lower cost.)

Governor Allen appointed Peter Schmidt, a Virginia citizen and successful businessman operating a regulated business, as director of DEQ, and charged him with bringing about a

192

streamlined, effective agency. Together, with input from DEQ professionals and concerned citizens, we set upon a course to decentralize this newly created department still operated at that time as four separate state agencies. Our purpose was to assure effective communication and coordination across air, water, and waste programs, and between the regulators and the regulated community. We established regional teams of permit writers and compliance assistance professionals closer to their clients. We believed functional consolidation and physical decentralization would result in greater and more immediate benefits to the environment, and we are being proven correct.

At the start of the process, more than 60 percent of the DEQ staff was located in Richmond, morale was low, and businesses complained about further centralization. Today, about 45 percent of the staff is in Richmond, morale is good, and businessmen generally say the system works better.

In carrying out this plan as we did, we achieved another important objective—we de-partisanized environmental politics; or at least we showed that we were willing to conduct policy in a non-partisan way. The plan we implemented was conceived and drafted in large part by Democrats in the legislature and the previous governor's office, and refined by career civil servants under the guidance of Schmidt.

Indeed, Schmidt, my agency chiefs, and I were able to cooperate with federal officials, and Democrats around the state, regardless of how strained the relationships became at times with our partisan foes. When the federal EPA needed help with a Superfund clean-up involving Greenwood Chemical in Albemarle County, they naturally contacted Peter Schmidt.

"We have a plan for shipping the waste out of the state to a site in Alabama," EPA's Tom Voltaggio explained. "But [Albemarle's neighbor], Nelson County, won't let us ship the waste through their district—meaning we can't get the waste" to Alabama.

Schmidt, thanks to his good relations with industry and with Voltaggio, was able and willing to piece together a plan. He knew that the rules for transporting such waste by train were different and more flexible than when shipping by truck. He also knew of a cement factory, run by Martin-Marietta, that had a major rail line running out of Albemarle County. With some retrofitting, it could ship the toxic materials out safely and at low cost.

Schmidt wrapped the package up and called Voltaggio back a few days later. Thus the Superfund program enjoyed one of its few successes—and Schmidt demonstrated his ability to get things done.

Some time after we left office, a researcher with the Alexis de Tocqueville Institution contacted Voltaggio, who had since become Deputy Director of EPA's Northeast Regional office. "You bet," he said, "Peter Schmidt made that happen and was very helpful to us. And that wasn't the only time he helped us out.... He helped us out of a lot of jams."

"Even though there were a lot of differences between our offices, we were able to work together. It shows you that attitude and approach are so important. He got beyond the rhetoric, and we tried to do the same. Even though I disagreed with the Allen Administration's approach on the environment, and still do, I would say Peter Schmidt and I accomplished a lot together."

There can be no higher praise than the grudging respect of a political opponent. In winning that respect, Peter Schmidt didn't stray one iota from the policy approach Governor Allen wanted. He was, in fact, carrying out exactly the kind of cooperate-with-everyone agenda that is at the core of Allen's populism.

W here federal programs were not working or threatened impractical and unnecessary coercion, of course we did not hesitate to oppose the federal government. We fought the California car plan and won—so completely that in the end, the Clinton Administration's EPA adopted our 49-state-car plan as its own. More than once, we took the Environmental Agency to Court—and won again.

Superfund, a failed federal program, was sent back to the federal EPA with the message that Virginia was not going to be an administrative arm of EPA, simply carrying out federal dictates. Superfund state employees were transferred into other positions while keeping a lean but effective team to be an advocate for Virginia's communities in any Superfund activities initiated in the state. Virginia's goal was to get land remediated and back into productive use quickly and cost-effectively, something the federal Superfund program has utterly failed to accomplish despite spending billions and billions of taxpayer dollars. Indeed, only two of thirty Superfund sites in Virginia had been removed from the Superfund list since its initiation in 1980 when I left office in 1998.

DEQ goals are now in place to reduce time for processing and issuing environmental permits, to cross train personnel and fully implement one-stop permitting, and to institutionalize the fiscal and personnel efficiencies promised to the General Assembly when it combined four separate agencies of government to create DEQ. Under the continuing leadership of Peter Schmidt's successor, Thomas Hopkins, we were constantly evaluating DEQ's performance with an eye toward new improvements and more efficiency for the taxpayer and the environment.

We established an emphasis on compliance as the most effective and efficient method of achieving environmental improvement under this new culture.

I appealed to Virginians' sense of pride in our special historical relationship with George Washington. In his Farewell Address, Washington had warned the new American nation to take care lest their national government become like fire, a "fearsome master," rather than the "helpful servant" everyone intended it to be.

It was my thinking that all Virginians, and especially civil servants to whom statutes had delegated authority over other citizens, would understand what Governor Allen and I wanted to accomplish if they understood that we genuinely believed in the sovereignty of the people. We knew that Virginia could provide better protection for the environment if all of us understood ourselves in terms of Washington's servants rather than his masters. It was my hope that such a change in the culture of the regulatory agencies would be more than cosmetic. It was intended to have profound consequences as to how Virginia government related to citizens, and was to be an important consequence of Governor Allen's Administration.

Today, regulators have a degree of flexibility in carrying out their statutory responsibilities, a reasonable system that even EPA now promotes. And the Allen Administration believed that most citizens wish to be in compliance with laws affecting their businesses. The role of DEQ can and should be to help these citizens comply with environmental laws, but should never engage in the perverse game of "gotcha" that epitomizes the fearsome master approach.

An analogy that I believe helps citizens better understand our perspective is to liken our compliance initiative to the "three strikes" concept. This does not mean that someone literally can ignore regulatory requirements up to three times. It does, however, mean that DEQ professionals will work with any regulated entity in a spirit of promoting compliance first. If, after DEQ has made and documented a reasonable effort to help someone achieve compliance, but that person is obviously a "bad actor" intent on defying the law and wantonly polluting, enforcement actions then occur. If people insist on violating laws, we refer them for enforcement action—hence our term "strike three and you're out."

This compliance-first initiative was highly successful. Virginia professionals were empowered to help a regulated entity achieve compliance through such measures as providing information and advice about investments in equipment upgrades and repairs, rather than in litigation, lawyers and fines. This is a win-win situation. The environment benefits, the government carries out its mission, and the regulated entity is in compliance with the law. Even President Clinton has now adopted the compliance-first policy as his own.

The Allen Administration implemented common-sense, science-based policies. We demanded benefit-cost analysis and insisted on input from locally elected officials and business and citizens affected as we established new policies. A relevant example is the Allen holistic approach to the Chesapeake Bay initiatives: toxics reduction, tributary strategies, nutrient reductions, and streamside management. On our watch, each environmental regulation promulgated or reviewed in Virginia had to stand the test of a review process with a set of clear, guiding principles suitable for specific situations to assure the result was real environmental benefits achieved in the most cost-effective and efficient way.

We acted on our conviction that regulations that are based on outdated science must be updated. All new regulations were required to undergo thorough review within four years. A scientific community that can discover new and exciting evidence from a rock fragment from Mars can certainly provide new scientific updates for environmental rules. No longer will Virginians be faced with outdated, outmoded, ineffective, and incomprehensible regulations that are process-oriented rather than result-oriented.

Science is based on accessible information that can be rigorously questioned and re-tested. Democracy, too, depends on "transparency"—information access so citizens know what the laws are, what their politicians are doing, and how they can change things.

Under George Allen, more and more information about environmental policy was provided not to an opaque priesthood of bureaucrats and "experts," but directly to (and by) average citizens of Virginia. We provided them with more direct access to important information about their natural resources and their environment.

At my direction and insistence the Natural Resources Secretariat developed home pages for each agency on the Internet beginning in 1996. I intended that each agency's site would work to achieve the kind of transparency and openness citizens should expect of their government. All regulations were to be made available in a format that will make them accessible to every Virginian with access to a computer. All public meetings were to be announced on the Internet and all public notices and proposed regulations were to be posted there.

And I directed that our Internet sites be designed so that communications between citizens, state and local officials and the regulated community would be interactive—so that these "clients" that the agencies in my Secretariat served could use the internet to provide feedback and other information to our agencies. Those were the early days of the net and it is impressive to see how Governor Gilmore has continued and expanded state government's accessibility through this communications tool.

Our opponents claimed that if these kinds of principles, policies, and practices were implemented, we would do significant damage to the environment. Even though the facts regarding environmental quality prove them wrong, I also believe their belief was genuine. It is hard to understand the fury and bitterness with which they lashed out at us otherwise.

In evaluating these claims, even on their face, it is important to remember the source. Though sincere, the commitment of some environmentalists to their beliefs is, demonstrably, extreme; to some even like a religious faith.

"We must make the rescue of the environment the central organizing principle for civilization," Al Gore has declared. "[That] means embarking on an all-out effort to use every policy and program, every law and institution, every treaty and alliance, in short, every means to halt the destruction of the environment."

Think about that—the central organizing principle. Not God or the human soul. Not justice. Not life, liberty, and the pursuit of happiness. With one stroke, Mr. Gore thus proposes to rewrite the Declaration of Independence. Specifically, he continues, writing virtually a decade ago, but reaffirmed in a 1999 edition of *Earth In the Balance,* "it ought to be possible...to accomplish the strategic goal of completely eliminating the internal combustion engine over, say, a 25-year period." What other products may have to fall under Al Gore's regulatory scythe?

Gore's protégé and my nemesis, Carol Browner, shared his disdain for gradual change and for scientific evidence. Announcing new regulations in 1994, she let her radical roots show.

"The current regulatory system is about going from A to B and B to C. The changes we undertake today are about going from A to Z," Browner boasted. "I don't think anyone in this country, whether environmental leader or corporate CEO, believes incremental steps will achieve the kind of future we all want."

Asked for scientific evidence on many points, Browner shot the messenger—alas, that messenger was often me—by savaging the motives of anyone who raised a hand and requested a study or a piece of data.

Zeal is in some ways laudable. It is even prudent, if circumstances warrant. But zeal is not science, even when it is wrapped in the mantle of science. It is, in fact, the antithesis of the scientific spirit, which is humble, self-critical, and patient in ascertaining the truth.

Ultimately, as economist Milton Friedman has said, the test of any model is its ability to predict. In such books as *The End of Affluence, The Population Explosion,* and *The Limits to Growth,* environmental extremists laid out in the 1970s, 1980s, and 1990s how our civilization is headed for ecological disaster. By this time, according to these models, the earth was supposed to be almost literally out of gasoline and other resources essential to the industrial consumer economy, and literally out of clean air.

Instead, air and water has improved worldwide—and it's gotten better faster in developed countries with free market policies. Food supply has outstripped even the most "optimistic" models of 1970s and 1980s famine-mongers. Prices of basic commodities, as free-market economist Julian Simon predicted in a famous wager he won with scientist Paul Ehrlich, have been flat, even mildly down, for a generation.

Human ingenuity, the natural resourcefulness on which our policies relied, has outstripped even the best laid disaster plans of ecological doomsayers.

When confronted with this kind of evidence, activist groups have a pat answer: The improvement is due to their activity and their staunch resistance to economic growth. When Alexis de Tocqueville called more than a dozen EPA officials in the summer of 2000 to ask for personal comments about Virginia's environmental record, not one would say the air, water, or soil were in worse condition than when George Allen took office. They merely wanted to give their own reasons as to exactly why things were better.

This is consistent rhetorically, but ignores an important part of the history: Those officials predicted things would get worse if we did what we said we would do. Well, we did it our way, and the environment improved. The burden should be on our critics to explain how their scientific assumptions went so far astray. Roy Hoagland of the activist Chesapeake Bay Foundation once commented, "The bottom line is that [Dunlop's] philosophy of environmental protection is counter to established environmental success, environmental science, and environmental political realities." What he could not say was that it was counter to environmental quality.

The height of absurdity was reached when Delegate George Grayson introduced a bill in Virginia's General Assembly to eliminate the Natural Resources Secretariat until I had vacated it. But the move backfired when the silent majority rose to our Administration's and my personal defense. The *Prince William Journal* suggested editorially:

> Among the most devoted and effective public servants in Richmond is a smart, classy lady named Becky Norton Dunlop, Virginia's Secretary of Natural Resources.

Largely due to Dunlop's tenacious battle with the ideological zealots running the U. S. Environmental Protection Agency, Virginians do not face the prospect of waiting hours in line at emissions inspection stations mandated by Washington.

Virginians also have Dunlop mainly to thank for the Commonwealth's enlightened refusal to join ill-advised campaigns by New York and Massachusetts, and their allies within the EPA, to force thousands of motorists in the mid-Atlantic states to buy the same costly electric vehicles of doubtful reliability and inadequate range from which California is now backing off.

Virginians additionally don't have to worry about their bosses watching over their shoulders every day to monitor their rush-hour driving practices under Washington's Employee Commute Options nonsense, thanks to the determined opposition of people like Dunlop.

Finally, there is the matter of Dunlop's insistence upon responsible environmental action designed to protect the Chesapeake Bay and jobs created by its treasures.

In short, Dunlop is fighting the good fight on behalf of Virginians' liberty and natural resources. She deserves praise and promotion from her fellow citizens.

So, naturally, James City Delegate George Grayson wants to fire Dunlop...Apparently, Grayson never saw a federal regulation or piece of red tape he didn't just love, even if it meant making Virginia motorists spend hours in line waiting for an emissions test that could just as easily have been done in the same service station down the road that does safety inspections...

Instead of being meanly harassed by the Graysons of the world, brave Virginians like Dunlop who are standing up to the federal leviathan on behalf of constitutional principle deserve thanks and commendation.

So get a life, George. And back off Becky.

It is revealing that in all these heated discussions of the environment, the environment itself became almost an afterthought. Not until we had been out of government more than a year, and that wonderfully vast "Clearing the Air" headline hit my e-mail, was there even much of a discussion by the political class about what was happening to the state's air and water.

But here—insofar as we know them in the summer of the year 2000—are a few facts about Virginia's environment and the trends in that environment as we left them in January 1998.

- Over ninety percent of Virginia's monitored waterways complied with Clean Water Act standards, compared to less than 70 percent typical of other states nationwide.

- Exceedances for ozone and particulate matter continued to fall in Virginia. Air quality advanced so much that by the time Governor Allen left office, only one area of the state was out of attainment with the Clean Air Act standards, compared with five that were not in compliance in 1993.

- The Chesapeake Bay showed measurable signs of improvement in virtually every regard. Interestingly, *E. coli* and other microbial outbreaks that seemed to trouble our neighbors, Maryland and the District of Columbia, have not yet been a problem in Virginia, even though our state was supposedly less protective of the environment.

- *Pfiesteria* that closed Maryland rivers in 1997, threatened the livelihoods of the Maryland fishermen and seafood purveyors, and became a bitter political issue, never was found to be a problem in Virginia rivers.

- Striped bass have made a dramatic comeback. Scores of bald eagles now roost along Virginia rivers and some previously seriously pressured species are so plentiful that hunting restrictions are repeatedly being relaxed so that the increased populations don't overwhelm their habitat.

- Perhaps most satisfying for me, people and businesses took upon themselves initiatives to clean up, recycle, and renew. The state's industries release fewer toxic chemicals than ever before. Businesses and residences were recycling more than ever. From Good Shepherd Church to the tree-planting strategies of Paddy Katzen, our state became a beehive of popular activism. And this personal-responsibility kind of activism has measurably improved Virginia's environment.

It would be wrong for me or the Allen Administration to take credit for all these developments. We were in office only four years. We followed years of increasing attention to the environment in the state and the country. We worked with others. On occasion, even the EPA helped out.

Most important, though, we demonstrated that citizens, not government, are the most significant engines of progress. It was not me, nor my agency chiefs, nor Governor Allen who cleaned up rivers and waste sites, and reduced air pollution around the state. It was the people.

Given Virginia's unprecedented economic growth under Allen, and the streamlining of government we achieved, and the woeful predictions of our critics, it should be considered a miracle that the environment didn't greatly worsen.

No one said, in the hot days of 1995 and 1996, that Virginia's environment was "going to get much better, but the Allen Administration's policies would slightly diminish the rate of improvement." Instead we were accused of "gutting" air safety standards, "fouling" the waters, and "promoting" toxic dumping.

If words are to have any meaning, how could we have "gutted" air standards if air quality improved?

According to Delegate George Grayson, Becky Norton Dunlop is "a wild-eyed radical, aligning herself fully with the degradation of Virginia's natural resources."

Well, considering that Governor Allen and I implemented nearly every one of the policies Grayson opposed, how is it that Virginia has even survived, let alone shown such improvement?

The fact is, the entire Allen team and I demonstrated that people of conservative persuasion can be successful in establishing and carrying out effective environmental policies. The principles upon which we based our success were articulated by me every time I had the opportunity, from my first day until my last day as Secretary.

These principles apply to Virginia, and to all states and jurisdictions. A Cabinet Secretary is called upon to give countless speeches, to make brief talks and introductions of other people, and to write articles. Never did such an opportunity present itself when I did not mention at least one, and almost always all five of my "Guiding Principles" in a context appropriate to the occasion. One such occasion was when the *Virginia Town and City* magazine, the organ of the Virginia Municipal League, asked me to pen a brief article early in our Administration. Here is what I shared with this publication, and with thousands of other Virginians during the course of the four years of the Allen Administration.

1. **People are our most important natural resource.** Is our work benefiting the people we are committed to serve? How can Virginians work together to develop solutions to problems?
2. **Personnel is policy.** We want to benefit from and make the best use of the diverse talents of the dedicated professionals in government, academia and in the private sector.
3. **A growing economy and a healthy environment are mutually dependent.** Private property rights and responsibilities, incentives of the market place, and the free

204

enterprise system offer the greatest new prospects for improving environmental quality.

4. **Renewable natural resources are inherently dynamic, resilient, and responsive to conservation management.** Proper and effective public policy uses deeds of good stewardship and the art and science of conservation management to improve the quality and condition of natural resources.

5. **Excessive federal mandates and regulations are injurious to the environment.** People and states—and local governments— have a responsibility to collaborate to challenge excessive and injurious federal policies and to devise ways to assure that the art and science of natural resource management and protection are applied in site and situation specific ways to assure improvements in environmental quality.

"Everyone looks to Virginia," Patrick Henry once said, "for examples."

The ideas that George Allen implemented were considered revolutionary when Virginia undertook them in 1994. Today, they are becoming more commonplace. I think we had something to do with that, and I take satisfaction. We helped indirectly, by showing market-oriented environmentalism based on the helpful servant, compliance-first model for the government's role can work. And we helped in a tangible, direct sense, by proving to other states that they don't necessarily have to cow-tow to whatever the EPA ordered them to do when they believe EPA to be wrongheaded.

"If you are running for office in Montgomery County, Maryland," wrote the *Montgomery Journal*, "would you stand meekly by as Carol Browner and Michael McCabe tell your constituents when and where they can drive their cars, mow yards, and build new homes and businesses? The answer, of course, is no way, even if you really would rather just sit back and ask 'how high' whenever the EPA says jump, which has been the attitude of too many Maryland officials for too long."

"What is really happening here [in the case of Virginia] is the EPA trying to make an example out of a state whose officials have successfully challenged the agency in federal court and thereby pricked a small but significant hole in that federal leviathan."

After Virginia stood up to the EPA about emissions testing, Congress and the EPA changed the requirements to allow other states to use the plan we had promoted. Because, in a lonely role among the states, Virginia opposed the imposition of the "California Car," the 49-state alternative pushed by our Virginia team became the national model. If imitation is indeed a compliment, Virginians should be flattered. Other states were doing some of the very things we had done first.

One of George Allen's particular kindred spirits was Texas Governor George Bush. He also insisted environmental decisions "be based on sound science and a thorough cost-benefit analysis," believed the best way to achieve clean air and water was "to work with local jurisdictions using market-based solutions," and rejected traditional "command-and-control" environmental protections. Indeed, one of Bush's first acts as governor was to appoint to the Texas Natural Resources Conservation Committee Ralph Marquez, a chemical engineer—signaling Bush's determination to have environmental decisions made by scientists, not ideologues.

"We have high standards," Bush said, "but we are also proving that government and citizens and business need not be enemies in the work of safeguarding our environment." Naturally, Bush came under assault from some of the same forces George Allen faced in Virginia. "We believe the air crisis is due to the intentional acts and conscious indifference of Governor Bush, his appointees to the Texas Natural Resource Conservation

Commission, and the legislature," commented Meg Haenn of the Texas Air Crisis Campaign.

The facts, though—there they go again—suggest that Bush has taken the environment more seriously than many of his predecessors.

For instance, when his state passed its Clean Air Act nearly 30 years ago, the law did not require existing industries to obtain air emission permits. The lawmakers believed it was more reasonable to exclude extant operations under a grandfather clause than to force expensive reconfigurations. For 25 years, no one questioned the wisdom of allowing nearly half the state's industrial plants to operate exempt from environmental-compliance laws—until Bush did in 1996. Deeming it unacceptable for outdated, unlicensed smokestacks to produce one-third of the state's industrial air pollution, Bush supported and signed into law remedial legislation.

Texas now leads the nation in the reduction of toxic pollutants. A *New York Times* analysis of Bush's environmental record, written by Jim Yardley, reported that environmentalists find this statistic "misleading," but doesn't say it's inaccurate. Texas, it might fairly be noted, has high levels of toxic pollution, but then, most of what went into that record reflects policies in place before Bush took office. From 1995 to 1999, Texas reduced air pollution 10 percent, and toxic pollution by 15 percent. The Bush administration also shepherded a change in Texas law to require power plants to cut their emissions in half by 2003, a step taken by only two other states—Massachusetts and Connecticut. Through 1998, the state was on target every year to reach that long-run goal.

Marquez says, "When he (Bush) appointed me, he said, 'I want decisions based on good science and to leave Texas cleaner than when I found it.' We've tried to deliver on that."

Like Virginia, Illinois has now set up a program offering small businesses help in complying with regulations and relief from penalties if they corrected problems. Ohio created a voluntary-action program allowing private parties to clean up contaminated sites.

Illinois, Minnesota, and Wisconsin entered into Memoranda of Understanding with the EPA about Superfund, overseeing clean-up and eliminating unfair liability. Michigan also amended its laws to hold an owner responsible for clean-up costs only when the owner contaminated the site. New York developed a clean-up program in which volunteers could investigate a site, clean it to an agreed-upon level, and the state would issue a "no further action" letter.

F rom the very beginning of my service to the Commonwealth, I believed that our success would depend on the degree to which our Administration could involve people in taking personal and individual responsibility for stewardship of Virginia's natural and historical resources. My experience as Assistant Interior Secretary for Fish, Wildlife and Parks had made me all too familiar with the "tragedy of the commons" mentality that had been the consequence of everyone assuming that environmental quality was somehow "the government's problem."

Also, as I traveled the state and had the opportunity to talk with and listen to parents and teachers of school age children, I became concerned that the "fear mongering" that is one of the principal strategies of environmental activists and government agencies always trying to justify more laws, "mission creep," and more grant money was very frightening to children. It seemed to me that one of the things we could do to add some balance to the common fare of frightful messages that always seemed to be associated with environmental matters would be to give Virginians some encouragement that they, as private citizens, could make a difference.

One element of this more optimistic and positive approach was our decision to initiate the springtime "Operation Spruce-Up" and a "Fall River Renaissance" to give local citizens, service clubs,

208

student groups, scouting programs, and all other sundry folk occasion to participate in community activities to improve and protect environmental quality. These programs were very successful, and continue to this day.

Another element of our positive approach was to produce some helpful guides. My office worked with all eight of my agencies and with other departments of Virginia government, such as the Department of Forestry and the Department of Transportation, as well as with private organizations. Together we developed two nifty little brochures. One was entitled "25 Ways to Help Virginia's Environment." Another, published in conjunction with the Fall River Renaissance program was entitled "20 Ways to Help Virginia's Rivers." These proved very popular, and are still in wide circulation.

In the long run, these kinds of initiatives by states and people can be a powerful dynamic for further environmental progress.

Imagine if, instead of fighting against the states, the federal Environmental Protection Agency encouraged experimentation and diversity in carrying out environmental statutes?

The EPA could almost become a clearing house for different approaches to common problems, and base its implementation regulations on what is proven to work.

An EPA that was transparent, rather than opaque, that welcomed peer review of its models, tests, data, and conclusions —would be a robust institution indeed.

It would probably, in a very short time, be much more truly pro-environment than it is now, with its spasms of enthusiasm for global warming this year, *E. coli* bacteria the next—running around like a headless chicken, proclaiming the sky is about to fall and kill us all.

In Virginia, we took a different approach than the EPA. By our fruits, we should be judged. It is a judgment we welcome.

"Virginia's environmental health declined until 1994, then started improving," the *Richmond Times-Dispatch* reported in a story about a Virginia Commonwealth University study in 1999.

If our policies didn't cause that outcome, I feel confident that they contributed to it, and at least got out of the way so the people of Virginia could.

Acknowledgements

There is a wonderful abundance of ways in which Virginians demonstrated during George Allen's term as Governor that a growing economy and an improving environment go hand in hand.

Deciding which experiences and episodes to relate and which to save for another time has not been easy. I have so many more inspiring stories to tell.

Many, many Virginians were involved in making our State a better place to live, work, and raise a family from 1994 to 1998. Hundreds of citizens gave me support and encouragement in countless ways like visits, letters, phone calls and with prayer during my tenure. I shall always remember and be inspired by these good people. They made my service rewarding.

A special thanks is due from me to those who served in Virginia state government and were part of our team to make government more responsive to its citizens and involve more Virginians in the wise stewardship and enhancement of our natural resources. My agency chiefs and personal staff contributed tremendously to my successful tenure because they were outstanding in their jobs. Peter Schmidt, Kathleen Lawrence, Tom Hopkins, Bill Pruitt, Bill Woodfin, Steve Pike, Michael Clower, Brian Mannix, Hobey Bauhan, George Lee, Kathleen Kilpatrick, Alex Wise, Richard Jefferson, Mike Costigan, Paddy Katzen, Julie Overy, Betty Joyner, Tim Cox, Karen Ramey, and my Governor's Fellows Greg Crist, Heather Wood and Eileen Guertler all served me with excellence and Virginia with distinction. Many current and former staff members in the Department of Environmental Quality, the Department of Game and Inland Fisheries, the Department of Conservation and Recreation, the Marine Resources

Commission, the Chesapeake Bay Local Assistance Department, the Department of Historic Resources and the Museum of Natural History were invaluable in the successful implementation of our policy initiatives. There were others, of course, but it is impossible for me to name them all. Individuals in Departments including Transportation, Agriculture, Health, Economic Development and Public Safety were key to many unheralded achievements. I was also privileged to serve with Cabinet members who became valued colleagues, advisers and friends.

George and Susan Allen are special people without whom this story could not be written. Principle, integrity, leadership, vision, values—these words come to mind when I think of the Allens. Their commitment to Virginians and the liberties Virginians have fought for throughout our nation's history inspires me still. Ronald Reagan, one of my heroes, also deserves mention for he reminded us that "There is no limit to what a man can do or where he can go, if he doesn't mind who gets the credit."

I am especially indebted to Gregory Fossedal Chairman of the Alexis de Tocqueville Institution for encouraging me to write this book and supporting the project. Jonathan Kavner, Sahir Zuberi, Ken Brown, and others I cannot name contributed enormously to this project. Without them, it would not be a reality. Gregory (and George, my husband) were the best counselors and editors I could have had.

The Heritage Foundation where I serve as Vice President has generously supported this endeavor and I thank Ed Feulner and my colleagues for their patience and encouragement. I particularly would like to thank Jon Garthwaite, Tom Hinton, Bridgett Wagner, John Hilboldt, Teri O'Neill, Rich Brink, Eric Korsvall, John Dickson, Kate Pomeroy, Ryan Zempel, Chris Cardon, Tom Scerbo, Lynn Gibson and Allegra Dryden for their support. They carried out our responsibilities for strategic outreach and

212

communication of conservative ideas even when I was focused on this book.

God has blessed me with tremendous opportunities and challenges, wonderful and generous friends and colleagues, a loving and supportive family and a creation that is majestic, dynamic, and a joy to steward.

We would especially like to thank the Charlotte and Walter Kohler Charitable Trust for its support of the research and production of this important account by Becky Norton Dunlop, without which this book would not have been possible.

–Gregory Fossedal, Chairman
Alexis de Tocqueville Institution

213